Marketing and promotion will include a national media campaign, bookseller/librarian outreach, digital advertising, targeted newsletters, social posts, and giveaways.

FOR MORE INFORMATION, CONTACT:
Rachel Fershleiser, Associate Publisher,
Executive Director of Marketing
rachel.fershleiser@counterpointpress.com

THE MIGRANT RAIN
FALLS IN REVERSE

The Migrant Rain Falls in Reverse

A Memoir

VINH NGUYEN

COUNTERPOINT | CALIFORNIA

First Counterpoint edition: 2025

An earlier version of Chapter 2 was published as "The Migrant Rain."
Brick, A Literary Journal 107 (Summer 2021): 47–53.

Sections of Chapter 3 first appeared in "First Readers."
Grain: The Journal of Eclectic Writing 50.3 (Spring 2023): 64–68.

An earlier version of Chapter 4 was published as "Four Photos."
Malahat Review 216 (Autumn 2021): 11–18.

An earlier version of Chapter 6 was published as "An Acute Accent."
New Quarterly: Canadian Writers & Writing 159 (Summer 2021): 16–20.

An earlier version of Chapter 7 was published as "Waiting, Resolution."
PRISM international 60.4 (Summer 2022): 79–89.

Li-Young Lee, excerpt from "Visions and Interpretations" from *Rose*. Copyright © 1986 by Li-Young Lee. Reprinted with the permission of the Permissions Company, LLC on behalf of BOA Editions, Ltd., boaeditions.org.

Excerpt from *The Year of Magical Thinking* by Joan Didion. Copyright © 2005 Joan Didion. Reprinted with permission from Penguin Random House LLC.

From the book *The Odyssey of Homer*, translated and with an introduction by Richard Lattimore. Copyright © 1965, 1967 by Richmond Lattimore; © Renewed 1995 by Alice B. Lattimore. Used by permission of HarperCollins Publishers.

ISBN: 978-1-64009-673-8

The Library of Congress Cataloging-in-Publication data is available.

Jacket design by Nicole Caputo and Farjana Yasmin
Jacket images: Vietnam street © Design Pics / Alamy Stock Photo;
man on bicycle © RyersonClark / iStock

COUNTERPOINT
Los Angeles and San Francisco, CA
www.counterpointpress.com

Printed in the United States of America
1 3 5 7 9 10 8 6 4 2

For my mother

CONTENTS

PART I: WHAT'S REMEMBERED

1. Certainty   000

2. The Migrant Rain   000

3. Here   000

4. Four Photos   000

5. On the Back of a Tiger   000

6. An Acute Accent   000

7. Waiting   000

8. Houston   000

PART II: WHAT HAPPENED

9. A Made-Up History   000

PART III: WHAT MIGHT HAVE BEEN

10. The Last Emperor   000

11. Decision to Leave   000

12. A New Life Begins   000

13. Kill Your Father   000

14. Mother Narrator   000

15. Flights   000

16. Falling in Reverse   000

17. Chonburi   000

Acknowledgements   000

VIỆT-NAM CỘNG-HÒA

BỘ GIAO-THÔNG và BƯU-ĐIỆN

NHA LỘ-VẬN

BẰNG LÁI XE
TỰ ĐỘNG

Nha

SỐ: 038070

PERMIS DE CONDUIRE
DRIVING PERMIT

THE MIGRANT RAIN
FALLS IN REVERSE

Part I

WHAT'S REMEMBERED

1

CERTAINTY

I'M UNSURE WHEN THE IDEA took hold, but when it did, it wouldn't let go. Finding the refugee camp again became an obsession, wrapping itself around my consciousness like tendrils reaching for the elusive January light. I would lie in bed at night, my eyes closed, and map out the place in my mind. Our family's cramped living quarters behind a ditch by the red dirt road next to the soccer field across from the commissary. The large trees with hibiscus flowers blossoming in the sun. The tent where films were projected on hanging canvas. Rusty buses that chartered refugees away to new lives.

When sleep finally overtook me, I would dream of the open sky folding in on itself, children roaming through curtains of monsoon rain, my mother's slight, electric figure standing in line for rations. Me, a lightning rod, jolting awake. With the glare of the city sneaking in through cracks in the blinds, I sometimes couldn't tell if I'd made up the past, if the refugee camp in Thailand was ever real.

It had been decades since my mother, my siblings, and I fled postwar Vietnam and arrived at the refugee camps in Thailand, where we were processed by the United Nations and granted asylum. In a black-and-white photograph documenting our first moment as refugees, my mother holds a placard with the number BT001401. Her lips are pressed together, sealing tension. Shallow eyes bear exhaustion, like something inside her had been snuffed out.

Clipped to each of our collars is a number from one to five, my mother first, and me, the youngest child, last. No one is smiling, but everyone—except me—is dutifully looking straight into the camera to be captured on film. I am errant, my face turned slightly to the side, eyes downcast. Either I'm a child who can't follow directions or I'm already on a path away from the narrative given to me, searching for pieces of a broken story.

Every time I look at this photo, I want to reassure this new family that they will be all right, that they are safe. I think of my father, missing from the image, anxious to leave Vietnam and join us at the camp. He was still alive when this photo was taken.

One day, remembering this photo, I googled "Phanat Nik-hom," the camp we stayed in the longest, the final one in a series of camps. The first result I got was a Google Maps location that told me it was in Chonburi province, not far from Bangkok. In its place now were newly built military barracks and a government office surrounded by large patches of brown-and-green fields. I scrutinized the curling shapes of the Thai script and zoomed in on the tops of buildings that looked like tiny Monopoly pieces.

I followed a link to eBay, where someone was selling a T-shirt with an image of a young woman carrying a child on her back. Underneath the image were the words: "phanatnikom refugee camp—Thailand—1993." I put in a bid, but ended up losing to someone else. I wondered who this person was, living a parallel nostalgia to mine.

I downloaded a sixty-four-page master's thesis by an anthropologist in California and read about identity, community, and resistance inside Phanat Nikhom. When I finished, I thought to myself, Is *this* what it was like? I felt grateful that someone had documented the camp with such scholarly expertise.

I found a technical report on the groundwater supply for the camp and learned the location of wells, the quality of bedrocks, and the amounts of diluvial deposits.

I joined a Facebook group connecting friends who lived in and transited through the area. Late at night, I lurked at posts by strangers looking for people they once knew or reminiscing about a life that's no longer theirs. I went from one blog to another and saw images of women washing at cisterns, men with their arms around each other, groups of children giving thumbs-up for the camera, rows and rows of tiny makeshift buildings. All this looking fuelled my desperate imagination.

I didn't tell anyone that the refugee camp had taken over my waking life and animated my dream one. I was afraid my desire would become a broken spell. If I spoke my longing out loud, surely all traces of the camp would disappear, including my fragmented memories.

ONE EVENING, AFTER A DRUNKEN night out with friends, stumbling from one bar to another, I blurted to my partner—

"I want to go back."

We were walking home during the early hours of the morning. It was raining that strange horizontal rain, and we had no umbrellas.

"We're almost home," he said.

"No, no, I want to go back to the refugee camp in Thailand, return and see—"

"Oh."

"—what's there, what parts of myself I left behind."

We were almost sprinting as we reached the intersection, the traffic lights reflecting on wet pavement. My head was spinning.

"I'm almost forty. I'm scared I don't know who I am. How I've gotten here."

"Here?"

"This. Toronto. Dreaming in English."

"Why now?"

"I don't know. It's just—"

I sighed.

Everything I was saying felt fanciful and futile at that moment. Nothing about my words, my feelings, or the situation aligned. My life washed away in the falling rain.

My partner held my forearm as we walked side by side in silence, toward the dry shelter of home.

"Okay, I'll come with you," he said, with so much conviction at my rash outburst that the possibility of returning to the refugee camp became real for the first time.

Voicing my aching want out loud to my partner made it more bearable, made it exist beyond my inner self. And—just as I thought it would—the desire to return slowly disappeared. As soon as I eased my grip, the idea of the refugee camp slipped away like a stray balloon floating up into grey clouds.

I went back to the progressive routines of my work and social life. Preparing lectures for my classes at the university, where I taught English literature. Joining friends for dinner parties and movie nights. Watching the streetcar go by from a café window. Reading a good book in bed next to my partner. I took pleasure from simple housework like vacuuming, taking out the garbage, or washing the dishes.

I flew to Calgary, where my mother lives, to listen to her sing melancholic songs while working in the kitchen. To eat her food and sleep under the same roof as her again.

I took a trip to Mexico City in late summer and marvelled at the vibrancy of a place that reminded me so much of Ho Chi Minh City, where I was born. If my partner had asked me then—the both of us standing in the wide expanse of the Zócalo square—if I still wanted to find the refugee camp, I would have turned to him and said, *What camp? What are you talking about?*

I'm often ruminating on the past, staring down the long tunnel of memory. When this happens, the more I try to resist, the more the past grips me by the ankles, and then I fall backwards, hands and feet flailing in the air. But thinking about this particular moment in time—the summer of 2019, a moment before things changed—I now see that I can be swept away by the present too, that it's easy to be pulled along from one day to the next, further and further away from the past.

WHAT STARTED IT ALL—AGAIN—WAS DEATH.

What made the present, as it was then, unlivable was the untimely death of my best friend and mentor, Don.

Don had a way of pulling you into his confidence, taking you by the arm and whispering something only the two of you would get. I first met him when I enrolled in a graduate program at a Southwestern Ontario university, where he'd been an English professor for decades. A white immigrant to Canada from Trinidad, Don had that singsong island accent, which mismatched the looks he inherited from his German ancestors. He started his career as a Romanticist, writing a book on the English poet John Keats, but gradually began research on Asian North American literatures. He was one of the few scholars in Canada doing this work, and he'd agreed to supervise my thesis.

During our first meeting in his bright corner office, he'd asked if my family knew I was gay. His question came out of nowhere, shocking me as I rambled on about research topics and book titles. But this was Don—bold and curious, awkward and up close. I didn't realize it then, but thinking back, I understand it must've been his own unspoken queer sexuality that was on his mind. He must've been wondering how someone decides to come out to their family.

Once, we had lunch, and he was characteristically charming. He folded up his tiny glasses before fitting them inside a small tube, then dug his knuckles into his eyes. After a quiet sigh, he hunched his shoulders and started rubbing his upper leg vigorously with both hands. He took long, silent pauses in between sentences. "You're lucky that your generation can be gay so openly—" he began.

After he came out, at the age of fifty, we went dancing and vacationed with our partners. We told each other secrets, asked for dating advice, and checked out cute guys together. He drove me to IKEA when I needed bookshelves and had me over for Christmas dinners with his children. There was a twenty-nine-year age gap between us, and despite our tropical backgrounds and different life journeys, we'd found each other in the snowy landscape of Canada. Don was a soulmate, the closest thing I had to a father figure.

When I received the phone call from his partner telling me that Don had had an aneurysm, it was an unusually warm October afternoon. I saw the caller's name on the screen first, and the moment I picked up, I knew something was wrong: Don had had a pounding headache, he'd pushed through and lectured, he'd driven home, he'd made dinner, he'd collapsed into a seizure, he'd been taken to hospital, his head full of blood.

I started shaking—the sensation of being pierced by an icicle.

I asked if I could see him, but it was too late. The doctors were going to operate on his body in a few hours: cut him open, remove his organs—and put them into someone else.

When I saw him next, his ashes were sealed inside an urn. I held it in my hands. It was heavy.

AND THEN SOMETHING ELSE HAPPENED. In the midst of my grief—that throbbing deprivation that rearranges the mourner's body—another lurking death resurfaced.

Don's passing pricked at the open wounds of my past. It set off something I knew—indeed feared with every fibre of my being—was long overdue. For almost three decades, I'd managed to avoid coming to grips with my father's mysterious death while seeking asylum.

In 1989, my father packed his belongings and followed the same route that we, his family, took to get to the refugee camps in Thailand. Like so many refugees before and after him, my father lost his life in the open waters. His death had always been a fact of my life, but I'd never actually mourned him—never looked his death directly in the face and said, *Here, I am here.*

For years, I had made various mental negotiations with myself: I'll deal with his death when I'm in a better place, when I'm more stable, more secure, more mature. Perhaps if I just sidestep it at every opportunity, it might somehow go away on its own. If I delay it enough, working through his death will become a problem for the future.

But the future always arrives, sooner than anticipated and without warning. Attempting to mourn Don felt doubly hard because every feeling, every thought, every question opened up to more feelings, more thoughts, and more questions about my father and about the nature of death itself. Everything became entangled because both men left my life with the same abruptness—a boxer's illegal knock to the back of the head.

One moment they were in the world, and the next they were gone. I didn't have the chance to say goodbye or the gift of time to negotiate and pray, to imagine how I might reorient myself without them—only concussive questions and nowhere to turn.

I lost my father when I was a child, and, with Don's passing, I experienced that loss again as an adult. One death became two, and the two are now one.

ONE COLD AND WINDY AFTERNOON, an image shoved its way to the front of my mind: a block of ice sitting inside a round plastic basin.

The ice is slowly melting in the heat of the room, with mosquito nets hanging from the ceiling. Slippers are strewn one on top of another in the entryway. My mother, lying on her side, fans me into afternoon slumber, an elbow propping her up. A sliver of light cuts across our reclined bodies.

In the refugee camp, ice was a luxury. Ice was the gold we bought from nearby locals through an opening in the fence. I'm reminded that the border of the camp was not impermeable. Goods and things and people passed through gaps in the corrugated tin and barbed wire barriers, places where guards accepted a few surreptitious notes passed into their waiting palms.

Thinking about what happened to my father led me back to thinking about the camp, about how he never arrived. If it was possible to enter and leave that enclosure, then why couldn't my father? Why him? Why this outcome and not another?

I imagine him, in the middle of the night, lifting the corner of a fence and squeezing his head through first. I imagine him walking with light steps to where we are sleeping. I imagine him parting the mosquito net, then sliding his tired body next to our resting ones. I imagine the sounds of crickets. The brilliant orange sunrise.

And so, the refugee camp took up residence in my mind again. I began to make serious plans to return, looking into flights, accommodations, and, most importantly, the precise location of Phanat Nikhom.

My partner encouraged me, suggesting that we go the next summer, that we also travel throughout Southeast Asia. Go back to Vietnam, where I, at that point, hadn't been for over a decade.

The trip to find the refugee camp in Thailand became an entire journey, one that would carry the weight of my missing father, my refugee past, and my ability to continue living in the present. It took on a mythic quality—the magical act that would propel me forward and allow me to finally grieve.

BUT BECAUSE THE COSMOS HAS its own plans and cares nothing about our human need, the entire world shut down in early 2020. For months, a virus had been replicating itself inside human cells, moving from body to body, making the infected sick with severe flu-like symptoms. Circulating in the air, the virus travelled fast and far, reaching every corner of the globe in a matter of weeks. Deaths began to multiply at a dizzying pace.

I folded back into myself, feeling the insignificance of my own experience. Minimizing my own sorrow. Denying that leaden feeling in my chest.

But I've had to learn the hard way that it doesn't work to pit a personal experience, so embodied and immediate, against a social one, so grand and urgent. There has to be room for both, because the personal is the training ground for the social, and the social gives form to the personal. I had to figure out a way to make enough space for what I was going through if I was to be good or useful to anyone else besides myself, if I was to stay tethered to this life.

That was when, one evening, in a hazy confluence of illnesses—stomach pains, allergies, headaches, and skin rashes—I opened a blank document on my computer and started sketching with words an image of a man falling through empty space.

It took days for me to recognize that this man was my father, and that my task was to populate that space he was falling through with my own memories and desires, and in doing so, to make his fall from this life acquire some significance beyond another senseless refugee death, a nameless person disappearing from history.

It was a way, also, of saving myself.

I began to move, even though airplanes were grounded and national borders were shut. I travelled long distances across the years in my mind. I went to places overgrown with weeds and tangled roots, places that required hard-to-obtain entry visas.

I asked myself for permission.

Returns aren't just physical, I realized. They're also psychic and emotional. The past, the refugee camp, and my father had always been there waiting for me, if I dared to go further down that memory tunnel, to extend my fingers a little more and touch, with the tips, something like the truth.

I was chasing certainty.

I had become, at the core, simply a fatherless person looking for answers. But when I turned my gaze backwards, the first things I saw were bomb craters littering the landscape. Unexploded ordnances. Unmarked graves. Remnants of war.

I needed to revisit the Vietnam War—where my father fought and where my mother, my siblings, and I still live in its ongoing aftermath. The war ended before my birth, but its fighting shaped my life in ways I have yet to realize. To arrive at a personal resolution, I would have to trek through the ruins of many demolished lives.

Those who have been through war know that war scrambles our stories and timelines. Our fragile worlds. It leaves behind no continuity, no whole. Its legacy is mess.

To make sense of what happened to my father and to my family, I would need to bend memory, stretch facts, and conjure desire. Lay out all the contradictions.

I had to unstitch myself to make a story.

So, I fell into the past, grasping for some kind of coherence.

It felt like trying to hold on to the falling rain.

2

THE MIGRANT RAIN

"They're speaking Vietnamese," I say to my partner, who responds that they are often too loud in the morning.

It's the first time I become aware of the people living in the apartment above us, and I'm struck by a terrible longing. I'm reminded that I rarely speak my mother tongue. Listening to the sounds that once shaped my world, I feel like a stranger down below.

But it's not actually my neighbours who are speaking. The voices are coming from their television. I can't make out any words, although the inflection is instantly familiar to my ear. There's a crack spreading in the ceiling, a spot where the stucco has crumbled. Looking up, my longing is intensified because everything coming through inches of concrete is muted, arriving not as language but as stunted reverb.

Weeks later, I see an elderly couple leaving the building. I catch a word of Vietnamese—ở đây—and turn my head. It's a simple word that indicates a location, *here*. I follow them out into the street and through the grocery store. It's early spring, but they are both bundled up. The woman is in a puffy jacket and knitted scarf that covers half her face. The man has on an ushanka, his hands meeting behind his slightly hunched back. In the store, they stop to inspect the produce, picking up scallions and tomatoes, comparing prices. I'm intrigued by their presence in this part of the city, that they live in a condo on a street that has been described as one of the "coolest" neighbourhoods in the world, populated mostly by white hipsters and young professionals.

I make up my mind that they are the neighbours, and I try to imagine how they arrived here: refugees who've lived for decades in an old suburban house, close to others who speak their language, a house they've now sold because their children are grown and they're getting too old to climb stairs.

Seeing them disrupts the idea of a life I've built for myself, away from my family and away from the past. They're both the same height, and the way they move together down the aisle is an aching image of heterosexual domesticity, one that neither my mother nor I will ever get to experience.

Is this what a Vietnamese couple growing old together looks like? Is this what happens when you survive war intact? Is this the life you get to settle into when no one dies?

I exit the store and slip into the crisp air, confounded by how my day has been derailed and how the things I've lost come back in the ordinary shape of two small strangers.

THAT NIGHT, YEARNING FOR COMFORT, which stands in for something I can't exactly put my finger on, I look for a television serial from my childhood. I find *The New Heavenly Sword and Dragon Sabre* streaming online. Released in Hong Kong in 1986 and starring a baby-faced Tony Leung Chiu-wai, the epic follows an orphaned protagonist as he acquires supreme martial arts, going on to save first the wuxia world from nefarious machinations and then China from Mongol invasions. Adapted from Louis Cha's novel, the serial is dubbed into Vietnamese from the Cantonese original. I play the first episode, and it feels like a reunion. The storyline and I catch up. The voice-overs are long-lost family members. An old, forgotten world unlocks.

When I first came to Canada, I was forbidden from watching these serials, which my aunts brought home as cassettes from video shops in Little Saigon. "Don't waste your brain," I was told. The Vietnamese words would crowd my head, preventing me from letting in new English ones. To this day, I'm constantly wary of the limited real estate in my mind, and often forget too many things of great importance. Back then, I'd spend afternoons trying to recall the letters of the alphabet without singing the song out loud, while simultaneously pining to know if the hero would succeed in mastering the Eighteen Dragon Subduing Palms.

Binge-watching *The New Heavenly Sword and Dragon Sabre* now feels like a rebellious act. I want all the words to crowd my mind again. I'd happily erase Deleuze and Derrida to let them in. When I get to the part where the hero's parents commit suicide because other people's expectations are just too much and the world is a tangle of tragic impossibilities, I realize that the Vietnamese words I learned from martial arts serials are all about honour, sacrifice, heartbreak, revenge, and gallantry. Maybe my aunts were right: What good are these stories for a boy who will go on to live in a condo on Queen West in Toronto and teach university students how to appreciate literature?

What I learned is this: when the hero falls off a cliff, he never dies. He always returns with renewed purpose, a changed man. Midway through the series, when Tony Leung tumbles from a rocky precipice, he lands in a secret grotto. Inside that grotto is an ancient gorilla, and sewn inside that gorilla's stomach is the coveted Nine Yang Manual. With nothing but time, our hero contemplates the manuscript's contents. One day, using his new ch'i, he emerges from the grotto to see the morning light.

A fall is not an end. The return of those who disappear, who seemingly die, is inevitable. The hero's reappearance keeps the plot going.

• • •

MY FATHER IS NOT A hero, but he has fallen from our lives.

In the late 1980s, when my family decided to flee Vietnam, my father had been back with us for six years. Before that, he was interned in a Communist re-education camp for seven years. And before that, there was war.

He came back to my mother, who didn't get on an airplane to come to Canada with her parents and siblings but stayed behind to wait for her imprisoned husband. At a time when everyone scrambled to get out, she had no choice but to begin again in the ruins of war. She took care of her three young children, my siblings, first by peddling cigarettes in the street and then by buying and selling gold on the black market. She had to learn how to ride a motorbike to get away from the police. Those who ran on foot always got caught.

I was born after my father returned. But the life he'd known no longer existed. The nation he'd fought for had been wiped from the map. Those he commanded had left or died. His old fatigues burned. In this new Vietnam, a man like him was disposable.

For a long time, I couldn't imagine what he had gone through in that re-education camp. As an adult, I read another man's account, which is the closest I'll ever get to my father's experience. This man writes about spending long hours labouring in the fields, followed by political orientation and self-criticism every evening. He details the dark corner of a cell and the damp floor many men slept on. He describes starvation and the spreading disease of hopelessness. I wondered about the land mines my father had to clear or the trenches he had to dig. I imagine that, in the absence of food, he ate geranium leaves, lizards, snails, and cockroaches to survive. The beatings he received or the humiliation he swallowed. How all this bent his back and battered his mind, how heartbreak stayed with him.

All that he went through lives on in me, in the tense and aching body I've inherited. His unknowable experiences are what make my words possible. This is how my story, with its many gaps, continues.

My mother visited him, trekking days and catching several buses and trains to get to the camp. These visits were his sole reason for staying alive and hoping for another day. He didn't know how long he would stay in detention or when he would be released. Life went on in the outside world. I can't fathom what it was like for him to return to so much loss, a world so foreign. But he was also transformed: he couldn't protect what was inside him from those re-educated years.

From the first few years of my life and the last of his, all I have are hazy memories. There was no possibility of work for men like my father, so he stayed home and looked after me, rocking me to sleep, spoon-feeding me sweet rice, waiting for me by the gates in the afternoon when preschool let out.

One day, my father placed me on top of his shoulders. My legs dangled on either side of his neck. I remember him walking by a concrete wall outside our house and telling me not to touch the barbed wire. I remember filling balloons with water inside the house. I remember being told we must leave immediately. My father said, "Child, finish doing that when you come back home."

This is the last memory I have of him. On that day, my mother, my siblings, and I got into a truck, and that truck took us to the water, and in the water was a boat, and that boat took us to Cambodia, and in Cambodia we walked into the jungle, and on the other side was Thailand, and in Thailand was a processing centre, and after the processing centre was a refugee camp.

And this was how we fell from my father's life.

We were now in a camp, and he would have to make his way to us.

I don't know why he stayed behind. I've never been able to muster the courage to ask my mother. Not knowing what the other knows has been the bond between us.

I HAVE A PHOTOGRAPH OF him. His thin figure leans against a light-blue wall. He is wearing a pair of brown leather sandals, dark-grey trousers, and a white button-up shirt. His arms are crossed. Next to him is a big vase with long branches of yellow apricot blossoms, a symbol of good luck. It is Tết, the lunar new year. He is smiling and you can see his white teeth.

On the back of the photo, he wrote in Vietnamese:

Ảnh anh chụp ở nhà dịp Xuân Kỳ Tỵ—cười còn buồn quá em nhỉ. Mẹ con em là nguồn sống của anh—Thiếu vắng đời chẳng

còn thi vị. Em có hiểu cho anh oi?? Xa như thế quã đủ rồi–
Đoàn tụ tới nơi rồi. Yêu đời lên em nhé!

And then in English: "Your devoted husband."

I'm astonished to read these last three words. That he knew English never crossed my mind, although it makes perfect sense: he must've had contact with many Americans during the war. I brim with a brew of excitement and regret whenever I discover something new about my father. English is another thing we now share. I become just a little closer to him. If we were to meet again, would we be able to speak to each other in this language? Would my feelings be understood?

Deciphering the five short lines in Vietnamese is a struggle. As I attempt to read them, only some words reveal themselves to me, like pieces of a broken vase buried in the soil, his writing an ancient script requiring a Rosetta stone. What my father wants to convey is revealed only as dusty impressions, a shell of his genuine feeling. The photograph I hold in my hand and the quality of the pen's ink is so real, yet everything—the past, my father, and his meaning—is far away and unreachable. I go to Google Translate for help, but it too is inadequate. The grammar is off, the meaning imprecise. With advanced technology, and a grieving child's desire, this is the best I can decipher:

This photo I took at home during the beginning of Spring—
the smile is still too sad, don't you think. You and the children
are my source of life—without you life has no joy. Can you

understand me?? I've had enough of this distance—a reunion
is coming. Continue to love life!

The photograph is signed and dated February 24, 1989.

Shortly after, my father got into a boat to join us at the refugee camp. We never heard from him again.

And that was how he fell from our lives.

TWENTY-THREE YEARS LATER, MY SISTER calls.

"A man said he saw Dad in Saigon in 2005," she says over
the grainy line.

"That's impossible! He's dead," I reply.

Of course, we don't know for sure. There is no official record, no certificate, no body to confirm his death. And without
such things—without what the living call closure—the dead
can return without warning in any shape or form, at any moment in time.

During a high school reunion for Vietnamese refugees in
Texas in 2012, a man approached my aunt and said, "I know
your brother. How is he?" After her stunned response, he told
her, "No, I saw him when he was fixing up a house. I came
up to him and we chatted briefly. He was living with a woman
and seemed a bit strange as we caught up. I know the woman.
I'll give you her name." My aunt also asked him to draw a
map to the house. My cousin in Ho Chi Minh City got on her

motorbike and drove there. When she arrived, she met the woman, who immigrated to the United States years earlier but, as it happened, was back visiting family. She said, "Yes, I know him. He hung out with my brothers back in the day."

And that is it, that is all we know. What someone said to someone else. What was relayed to my cousin relayed to my aunt relayed to my mother relayed to my sister and then to me. And a crude drawing of parallel lines that became streets when labelled, a square that was supposed to be a house, a woman's name, and the year 2005, circled.

"He would never leave us for a woman," my sister says emphatically.

"So what do we do?" I ask.

My sister thinks we should speak directly with the man and the woman. My brother thinks the man is old and senile, someone who made up the whole thing or has mixed up his dates. My mother cries at night, everything she's repressed coming back. *Why did he abandon me and the children? Why doesn't he love me?*

Our family thrown into crisis by a man who thought he saw a ghost.

FOR DAYS, I CAN'T DO anything but stay in bed. One morning, I get up, wash my face, and dress. My sister emails me: "I know for sure he is no longer alive so what's the point of knowing the story." It is a statement and not a question. She's right. We decide to leave it alone. She adds, "Don't bring this up with Mom . . . just pretend you don't know. I don't want her to think about this any longer." We have to finally give the story an ending, and in the place of a missing body, we put down a single period.

After her husband's sudden passing, Joan Didion wrote about entering the time of magical thinking. For those who grieve, magical thinking is the insistence that the dead will come back. It's a stubborn hope, despite all evidence, that the clock will rewind so living can resume. The materials of the past have not yet moved, or indeed cannot move, into the past tense. The cold body's organs, the pair of shoes, last night's dinner, all hold out for the return of the deceased.

I've spent my childhood and much of my adult life drifting through the time of magical thinking. And yet I've never stopped to consider what my father's return might actually mean.

Didion asks, "If the dead were truly to come back, what would they come back knowing? Could we face them? We who allowed them to die?" Magical thinking has nothing to do with the dead and nothing to do with their return. It is the living's way of staying in the world, and that is a hard lesson to learn. If the dead came back, they would know nothing and we wouldn't know how to face them, we who allowed ourselves to live. We wish that the dead will return to us, but we don't consider that they might have nothing to return to.

If my father comes back to the house we once all lived in together, he'd find an entirely new family. The husband would politely greet him at the door and say, "The people before us left long ago. We hear they are in Canada now." The door would click shut and my father would walk away alone. Without direction in this new world, he would have no way of finding us.

MONTHS LATER, I FEEL AN intense anger. How could he leave? How could he let me suffer?

I crawl into bed, remaining there for days. I'm not sure how or when I'll come back out. But then I have a deadline to meet, and drinks with friends. My roommate makes me dal for dinner. I make plans to visit my best friend in London, to tell her everything in person. And just like that, life gets going again. When the opportunity presents itself, I don't go looking for my father. It's a betrayal of my devotion, but I feel, for the first time, that the void he left was not as large as I thought it was. It dawns on me that through the years I've somehow patched the edges of the gaping hole. Or learned to live around it, so life's fullness canopies over the absence it encircles. "He's no longer a part of how I live," I say to my friend when we fly from London to Warsaw. We both cry in the hotel room.

What comes after magical thinking?

• • •

28

IN 2004, MY MOTHER, MY second sister, and I return to Vietnam. My sister's husband comes with us. This is our first trip back since we left sixteen years earlier. We are tourists who trace the S-shape of the country, going from south to north, visiting cities, beaches, and historical ruins. What we see is a packaged tour for those who've been away too long.

During our last few days in the country, we decide, on a whim, to go to our old house. The taxi drops us off in front of a wet market. "This is as far as I can take you. There's no car allowed into those small alleys," the driver says.

We make the rest of our way on foot, passing stalls of green vegetables, hanging pieces of meat, and slabs of scaled fish. The bustle of prices and women haggling. Buzzing flies.

We arrive at a blue house that looks freshly painted. It's smaller than I remember. The concrete wall with barbed wire is still there. My memory expands: I see now that it fences off another row of houses, where other people live next to the memory I've long preserved.

I borrow my brother-in-law's camera and take photos of the house and everything that surrounds it. I don't want to have to rely on memory alone. As I'm clicking the button again and again, I feel a sense of creeping desperation, as if, in the next minute, it will all crumble into dust, and who I am will be swept away with it. I'm convinced that the photos will serve some crucial future purpose. One day, I'll show them to my nieces and nephews, or to the person I'll spend the rest of my life with. One day, I might sit down to write about this experience, even though everything will have been buried under other things by then.

Later, when my sister and her husband divorce, he takes the photos with him. Clearing out his old life, he will look at the photos and, seeing nothing of significance, throw them into the trash.

As we are leaving, a woman calls out my mother's name.

We turn around and she's approaching us with open arms. "Welcome home," she says. But we, with our backpacks and cameras and sunscreen, are nowhere near home.

"Long time no see. Are you good?" the woman asks.

Shocked, my mother embraces her.

"I could tell it was you from your gait," the woman says. Time has contracted, the past can really come around again. "A policeman lives there now," she says, pointing at the house. While we've been away, this woman has stayed put, continuing the life we left behind in the same house adjacent to the one that used to be ours. She says my mother hasn't aged a bit. Sixteen years crushed flat like a can of Coca-Cola. "What are you doing back here?" she asks. I don't know who she is, but she knows who I am. She puts a hand on my arm, and I understand that we are the ghosts who have reappeared on a random hot afternoon in the middle of a tiny alley.

BECAUSE THERE IS NO GRAVE that marks my father's resting place in this world, I don't know where to find him. A meeting with the dead can't be planned, a reunion always delayed. No flowers placed on a headstone. Instead, he wanders on a path I've carefully mapped out for him in my imagination. He's coming closer, I can feel it. He'll call out my name. I'll turn around.

Truth is, I don't dream of him, and no, he doesn't come back to me. Sometimes I struggle to recall what he looks like, a figure flickering in the blur of my mind. If what my mother says is true—that I resemble him—then the image that reflects back to me in the mirror is a negative that cannot be developed. One day, cheekbones will soften and lines will crack, and I too shall fade away.

In a poem, Li-Young Lee describes walking up a hill to visit his father's grave. After forty-one lines, and starting over again and again, he never arrives. The poem is about the difficulty of relaying what is true and accurate about our relationship with the dead. It suggests the impossibility of meeting with them, even if the grave is there, the chrysanthemums in our hands are real, and our longing is infinite. In the end, the poet writes:

And what was far grows near,
and what is near grows more dear,

and all of my visions and interpretations
depend on what I see,

and between my eyes is always
the rain, the migrant rain.

The migrant rain is what falls between the past and the present, the dead and the living. It is the screen through which everything that was is filtered. The years take on the glassy translucence of water. What we see are blurred shapes shifting in reverse. All our visions and interpretations as we turn back are moving outlines of other people. To live, we migrate in time, and to speak, we learn the language of rain.

FORTY EPISODES LATER, NEAR THE end of *The New Heavenly Sword and Dragon Sabre*, I hear the sounds coming through the ceiling again. I stand up on the couch, find my balance, and slowly position my computer under a vent. I turn the volume up—*click, click, click*—and press Play. Vietnamese words travel through the little slits, along a network of ducts, and into the home above. I know they are garbled or drowned out in all the darkness, but I hope the neighbours know that I am here.

3

HERE

Shortly after seeing my neighbours, the Vietnamese couple, I experience the most intense craving. I cannot identify it at first, just a rumbling in the stomach, a need for mooring and containment, like being swaddled tightly. I mistake this craving for literal hunger and make all the Vietnamese comfort foods I know how to cook—beef stew with hints of cloves and cinnamon, braised pork belly with coconut water, grilled chicken with lemongrass. But none satiate the ache.

I'm still a hungry ghost.

In the midst of this haunting, my mother calls from Calgary to check in on me. She wants to know that I'm not ill with the Covid virus, that I wash my hands properly and keep away from others in the street. She says she has repurposed her unused sheets to make face masks, which she's placed in zip-lock bags, wrapped in paper and packing tape, and mailed to me in Toronto.

She knows it's not possible, but she tells me that she wishes I could come home. Về nhà—literally, to return to the house.

That's when I, to my surprise, figure out the craving. The idea of home has always been suspect in my mind, a myth reserved for those who've never been displaced, who don't look like me, who grew up with both parents, who aren't queer. Home is something refugees and immigrants like me should want, and yet it remains just out of our reach. In the books I read, finding home is a refugee's purpose, and our problems are resolved by achieving "belonging."

But I've always preferred to stay on the sidelines, asking, What does it cost to belong? What vision is possible on the margins? Why is home also a cage?

And yet, in its defined sharpness, this disorienting murmur in my belly reminds me that I don't actually know where, or what, home is.

On the phone, I tell her, "Soon."

Soon, Mother, I will return to the house.

I WAKE UP EARLY ONE morning to find Toronto blanketed with snow. Overnight, a spring storm has passed through the city and turned it white like a blank page. Looking out the window of my apartment, I see a lone figure making first tracks in the snow, small markings that do not follow a straight line.

I recall reading somewhere that all immigrants to Canada have a first memory of snow; it is our introduction to the beauty and brutality of the country—and, like that, an image of me as a little boy cupping snow in my hands slowly takes shape.

It began at the Calgary International Airport, where aunts and uncles ran toward my family as we passed through the arrivals gate. Everyone huddled together in long-awaited hugs. My mother broke out in tears, and seeing that, I began sobbing too, not knowing the stranger who had lifted me up in his arms. Someone slipped a padded jacket over my shoulders and covered my hands in woollen mittens.

We were ushered into my grandfather's rusted Toyota Corolla, and he drove us to a four-bedroom bungalow cordoned off by a chain-link fence. This bungalow was my first home in Canada. Twelve people shared this house for many years. In those early days, there was no such thing as private space or personal secrets. We all knew when someone left or entered the house, we all ate the same thing, we all saw each other in our dreams and often resented such intimacy.

Being the youngest, I shared a bed with my mother in the basement. Every night, I pretended to be asleep when she came into the room, where my teenaged brother also slept, on his own bed in his own little corner. The waterbed wobbled when she got on, and I could finally stop holding my breath. I could let go of my fear of drowning and let slumber overtake me because she was nearby.

On that first day, when I got out of the Toyota, my grandfather urged me to walk over to the fence, crouch down, and scoop the strange dust into my hands. I held the freezing sensation. The snow melted and dripped through my fingers.

I HAVE ANOTHER MEMORY OF snow—my mother walking me to my first day of school. It was a complete whiteout that day, so we couldn't see what was in front of us. I wore my hand-me-down snow pants, and my legs made a swishing noise against the wind. It was so cold, my eyelashes stuck together, my burnt cheeks felt like they were cracking open.

When we arrived at the school, my mother handed me a piece of paper. "If you don't see me at the end of the day, give this to someone." She read out an address, a telephone number, and my name. "Everything they need to know about you is here." The essential parts of my new life folded neatly into a square.

I spent the entire day sitting alone at a desk, as I would for the rest of the school year. At some point, all the children gathered around the teacher, who was perched on a chair holding open a book. I didn't join them, remaining where I was with a piece of blank paper and a rainbow of broken crayons. I sketched a house with a chimney next to a large green tree, a yellow sun in the top right corner. It was not Canada, or the refugee camp I knew, but a generic image that every child learns to draw.

When I heard the bell ring, I stood up and got ready to go home. All the children rushed to put on their jackets, toques, scarves, and mittens. I followed them into the hallway but didn't see my mother. Panicked, I took the piece of paper from my pocket and held it out to someone taller. I saw their mouth moving, but the sounds did not reach me. I was about to cry—or maybe I did, maybe I sobbed out loud—and then suddenly I was sitting alone in an empty office with my head down.

Soon, a child my age appeared. Blond, sparkling eyes. He took my hand and led me to what I would later learn was the playground. I stood and watched the children hang from what I would eventually call "monkey bars," go down what I would one day spell out as *s-l-i-d-e*, and bounce on what I would always struggle to pronounce: a *seesthaw*. Everything was covered in snow.

I HAD NO WORDS OF English, but I remember that my second-grade teacher was Mrs. Brouillette. Her hair curled into short locks that did not bounce when she walked, and her thick glasses framed a bony face. She didn't know what to do with this child who wouldn't participate, who kept his head down all day. But she didn't push.

One day, I had to relieve myself but didn't know how to tell her. I held it in for as long as I could until I was about to pee myself—my thighs pushed tight together. I went up to her and pointed desperately at my crotch. I was embarrassed, but she was kind and held my hand all the way to the bathroom.

When I was in high school, someone recognized me on the public bus. She scooted into the seat next to me and said, "Vinh, do you remember how in elementary you swore at everyone?"

"That's impossible," I replied, "I didn't even know how to ask to go—"

"Yes," she interrupted, "we tried to befriend you, but when we got close, you'd shout, 'Fuck you!' and then mime some badass kung fu moves!"

"No—"

The mortified look on my face made us both burst into unstoppable laughter.

I still have no idea where I learned those swear words. If I follow the trail back, I might remember the two boys who stalked me on my walk home from school, making rude noises and stretching their eyes. I might see that one afternoon I pushed them both into a snowbank, screamed words I didn't understand, and then ran until the cold air stung my lungs. I might hear a family member teaching me the right pronunciations, the hard *f* sound and the short, guttural emphasis.

I eventually acquired more words of English that first year, mainly from watching shows like *Inspector Gadget* and *Tiny Toons*. They were innocent words: *uncle, helicopter, rabbit, run,* and *matter*. At school, I kept to myself, lived in my head, hoping that no one would discover my hideout. During recess, I'd act out the martial arts serials I loved in the wide-open schoolyard.

A kick here, a hand chop there, a leap into another time-space. *Hiya!*

The fact was, at age ten, I hadn't had any formal education. I spent some of my most formative years roaming around in the refugee camps, preoccupying myself with children's games. My childhood had provided me with a sense of play and free time, but I could not read, could not tell time, could not do multiplication. I didn't know how to study or how to learn.

The only thing I did at school was draw.

At the end of that first year, Mrs. Brouillette handed me a certificate and told my mother I was quiet and well-behaved.

IT'S A WONDER, I SOMETIMES think to myself, that I ended up becoming a professor. That kid who hated school, who struggled to learn, is now teaching others. He's still present somewhere inside me, sitting in a corner of my psyche, drawing figures flying through the air, martial artists shooting fireballs from their palms. His existence is why, every time I'm in front of the classroom, I still feel like a ten-year-old, puffing up my chest to appear older, stronger, wiser.

I left home for the first time when I was twenty-three years old, crossing the Pacific Ocean to teach English in Tokyo and reinvent myself as an adult. But leaving Canada was how I ended up becoming *Canadian*.

After fourteen years in Calgary, I had never once walked down a sidewalk with confidence, as if I had the right to be there. I'd always move aside to let those who belonged pass. I marvel at it to this very day—that unaware, unearned, blissful ownership—when I encounter it embodied in the flesh of many casual pedestrians. Now I think to myself, What does that feel like, and what does that person miss out on when they move through the world in such a fashion?

In my teens and early twenties, I lived in the northeast "ghetto" of the city, full of Black and brown kids who ate curries and jerked goat. We weren't supposed to make it out of there, or make anything of ourselves. Pretending to be hard was our pastime. My closest friends were immigrants and refugees from Cambodia, Laos, and the Philippines. We skipped school, played pool, and smoked cigarettes, enjoying the life our parents worked so hard to give us. But none of us knew what it meant to be Canadian.

When I moved to Japan, I had to keep telling people I was from Canada—"Yes, really, *Canada!*"

One time, I had a lesson with a precocious seven-year-old Japanese student. The first question she asked was "Where you from?" After I answered, she kept pointing at me and saying, "Yellow, yellow." I was confused until she, exasperated, reached across the table to touch my black hair and repeated, "Yellow."

She couldn't comprehend a Canadian who looked like me and like her.

I chuckled and tried to explain who I was as best I could with simple vocabulary. I pointed to a map hanging on the wall:

I was born here and went here and grew up here and moved here and now live here.

More confused and dissatisfied, she brought her fingers to her eyes and stretched them out, a smile on her face—a demand to account for myself, coming from a girl who shared the same skin tone as me, the same eye shape. This gesture brought back so many memories of growing up in Canada. But, in this country, what could I do but also bring my fingers to the corners of my eyes, stretch them, and stick my tongue out at her.

THE WEEKEND AFTER MY INTERACTION with the little girl, I went with friends to Ni-chōme, Tokyo's gay district, and drank my Saturday night into oblivion. I felt free to do and be what I wanted. In my blissful youth, I didn't have to think about nationality, race, or desire. I was no longer constricted by my past or who I once was. I was just another sweaty body in a dancing crowd, engulfed by fake smoke and whirling lasers. I met a blond Australian and we spent most of the night making out in the bathroom.

At dawn, we stumbled onto the platform of Shinjuku-sanchōme Station. We couldn't stop kissing each other. We didn't care that we'd been up all night. We didn't care that it was six in the morning and those waiting next to us—in ironed suits, holding packed cases—were on their way to work.

I pinned him against a pillar and stuck my tongue into his warm, eager mouth as the tunnel filled with rushing air.

Everything swirled as our saliva mixed. It didn't matter when the train came or where it was going.

I can't think of Tokyo without seeing the interlocking trains, like veins and arteries keeping the city alive. I saw a film once in which the main protagonist wandered the city recording train sounds, haunting the central Yamanote Line. He saw the looping train as a nurturing womb that held orphaned souls like him.

The first time I rode the Yamanote, I wanted to get off, but then the doors slid shut before I could change my mind. The buildings outside, haphazardly stacked on top of each other, blurred past me as the train picked up speed, humming as it carried me and everyone on board around the city centre.

I was alone, without friends or family, and I was about to arrive at Shibuya, the busiest place on earth. All I had was a map of the train system, which looked like the mad master-piece of a child discovering crayons for the first time, coloured lines scrawled across the page, intersecting and looping before dropping off at the edges. I held it in my trembling hands and looked up to see people absorbed in their own quiet lives.

Not knowing what else to do, I sat down on an empty seat. Beside me a salaryman in a grey suit hugged his briefcase. His eyes were closed, his head lowered and swaying to the train's motion. Across from me a young woman sheepishly pushed a

THE MIGRANT RAIN FALLS IN REVERSE

small piece of rice ball into her mouth, an act that, I would later learn, breached etiquette.

As I sat there, I was lurched out of time, thrown decades back into another moment of departure. Or it might have been a moment of arrival, I couldn't tell.

I'm five years old and I'm sitting on my mother's lap. We are cradled inside a small boat with other bodies crammed into us. It's dark so I can't tell where the water begins and the sky ends. Our limbs become one, our boat blending into sea. There is no sound in this memory, even if the surrounding water roars.

When the train reached the next station, the doors jerked open, and passengers spilled into space that—just moments ago—was empty. I was again crowded by others, pulled along in a rush toward a womb of skyscrapers.

When I left Vietnam, I didn't know I was leaving home. Because our escape was secret, my family could not risk an indiscreet child leaking the plan to neighbours or teachers who might in turn report these plans to authorities. So I had no idea what was happening. I didn't really leave home as much as I had it yanked away from me.

But leaving my home in Canada and coming to Tokyo was a choice I made, and I sat there fearful of getting lost. I looked around the train and wondered where all these people were going.

• • •

MORE THAN A DECADE LATER I'd find myself back on this train in a recurring dream: I've returned to Tokyo and time is running out. I must visit all my old haunts, the places that shaped me, and keep vigil so the flame of memory won't extinguish. To get there, I board the Yamanote Line, but sometimes the train is going the opposite direction, sometimes it doesn't arrive, sometimes I end up elsewhere. Once in a while, I get to my destination and my purpose is to take in as many of the sights and sounds as possible, stow them somewhere oblivion cannot touch.

When I wake up, it's not just the city that has begun to disappear. The dream itself becomes a water stain that can only be seen from a certain angle of light, drying up before anyone notices it was even there.

I don't want to belong to a place, but I want a place that belongs to me.

OUR HOUSE IN HO CHI Minh City was a narrow two-storey building shaped like a matchbox, grey concrete with a small balcony. On the ground floor was the living room and kitchen. On the second floor were two rooms, but I remember we only ever used one, laying mattresses on the floor so everyone could sleep together. The house, one French philosopher claims, is where a person's dreams are made, but I think he understood that dreams break there too.

In 1988, my family could no longer stay in the house because postwar Vietnam was not for people like us, citizens of a fallen nation. When Communist forces entered the city more than a decade earlier, the inhabitants became both stateless and prisoners. They were a population to be disciplined into a new nation-state, a new way of belonging. My parents applied for exit visas. They waited for entry visas. Relatives filled out paperwork to sponsor us. We filled out paperwork to be sponsored. For years we remained stuck in one place.

My parents eventually decided that it was time to leave, to cross the border on our own. Years of imprisonment, hustling in the black market to make a living, and a futureless future had stunted my family. We were not the first ones to pay smugglers for a way out of the country, and my parents knew there were no guarantees. The police patrolled the waters daily, looking for people trying to flee.

Those who were caught were sent back.

Or their boats were capsized in the middle of the sea.

Or they were executed on the spot.

Our life in Vietnam wasn't the one we wanted, but it was not nothing. So it was decided that my mother would take the four children and leave first while my father stayed behind to guard our life, in case we still needed it. Authorities lay in wait to occupy the empty houses of those who left. Many failed escapees came back homeless.

I have a memory: My mother and father are lying in bed. I crawl over their limbs, reaching across my father's face to remove his right arm, bent and resting over his forehead. I know that it's a gesture of worry, and I don't want that for him. My parents talk cryptically, so I can't understand. But I can sense what they are feeling, the scent of uncertainty stifling the room.

Shortly after this memory, I lost my first home forever.

As I sat on the Yamanote my first day in Tokyo, humidity in the air, I felt something I still have no language to adequately describe.

Something was ending and something about to begin.

"I DON'T WANT TO LEAVE," I protested when my mother came back from a long-awaited meeting with Canadian immigration officials. A different life was being prepared for me and my family in another country, and I was frightened, trying to hang on to what I knew.

By that time, we'd been in Thailand for three years, moving through three different refugee camps, which were the most stable places in my young life. I didn't realize that refugee camps were only meant to be temporary, not a home, but a place to transit through.

Before the war had officially ended, my mother's sister and her husband had had the foresight to leave. They went through the refugee camps before these camps became bottlenecks, places where asylum seekers languished. Through my aunt's sponsorship, my grandparents and all their children, except my mother, secured seats on an airplane and headed for a place called Alberta.

My grandparents arrived in Canada and set up home in a large trailer park in the small town of Airdrie, where they all worked on a mushroom farm, picking creminis and portobellos. My grandma wrapped plastic shopping bags around everyone's shoes before they walked to work in the snow, because that's how an immigrant finds a way to stay dry.

While we lived at the refugee camp, my grandparents saved their mushroom money and began the paperwork to sponsor us.

"In Canada," my mother said, "we will have our own house, with rooms, and in the bathroom the shower will bloom like the head of a lotus. Warm droplets will fall onto your body." That, she said, was the feeling of happiness.

But I wasn't convinced. For me, happiness was the monsoon rain that made a copper-coloured river out of the dirt roads, deep enough for me to pretend to swim all the way home.

The choices others make often amount to a life, and in 1991, I arrived in Calgary.

IN MY MIND, CALGARY IS always frozen under layers of that strange white dust, and the one memory of snow that will forever remain crystalline is the day my mother said she would deliver a McChicken sandwich to my elementary school. She promised me. But when I looked outside and saw the blinding snowstorm, I knew she wouldn't show up. At lunchtime, I sat around with my friends in the giant gymnasium, joking around, drinking a small carton of milk, telling them I forgot my food at home. By this time, I was in sixth grade and had enough words to explain away these kinds of complex situations.

As lunch came to a close, one of the supervisors, in her blue smock vest, called my name and told me to come with her. I thought someone had noticed my lack of food and reported it. I thought my mother was going to be in trouble. We were walking toward the principal's office when I saw my mother standing in a corner, covered head to toe in snow, holding with both her hands a brown bag with the golden arches on it. The bag was so wet it looked like it was about to disintegrate.

Then she said in a small voice, "Mother is here."

I'VE BEEN PONDERING WHAT IT means to be here. Here is my apartment and my life with my partner in Toronto. But I know that here is much deeper than the lived surface. Here, I suspect, is constantly shifting. Here is almost forty years of a life that cannot be tallied in linear time or measured with teaspoons. Here could be the city of my birth long forgotten. Here might be a state of mind ready to journey back to the past. Here might be staying put even with the stinging ache of regret. And here might be mistaken for home, but don't make that mistake, because here doesn't need something so easily desirable.

What here requires is the traffic in between the space where home is lost and when home becomes possible.

TWO YEARS AFTER LEAVING TOKYO, I returned to the city, the first home of my choosing. Everything seemed the same, but I was different. I made plans to meet with old friends, and one evening, as I entered the train station with its talking machines and bustle of commuters, I was struck with the saddest feeling. It was as though I had suddenly faded into a ghost. It was like I'd been late to the world this whole time, everything already over.

Two years prior, I could've navigated the trains by instinct—knowing where to get on and off, when to make transfers, the names of different lines—but now I stood there dumbfounded, not knowing where to go or what to do. The tinkle of the train doors closing danced from my ear to my heart and down to my belly, becoming trapped there. What was once second nature—embodied knowledge of a place—had become confusion and fear.

I can't tell you what the feeling of home is like, but I can tell you the feeling of having lost it. That's the only feeling I trust.

4

FOUR PHOTOS

A CACHE OF PHOTOGRAPHS ARRIVES in my inbox. When I open
the compressed files, image after image appears, like brilliant
fireflies giving form to the night. They number in the hundreds,
downloading in rows and rows that overwhelm my inadequate
human eyes. I need to catch my breath before I actually look at
them, and when I do, I see images of my family, dating from the
1950s all the way to the present.

My brother-in-law, my eldest sister's husband, has under-
taken the monumental task of digitizing our family albums.
Each photo a story of how my family came into being.

I spend hours and hours clicking through the images on my

screen, moving through space and time in the small confines of my living room.

In one sitting, I see my siblings grow from children to adults with their own children, and it's an unsettling experience. I realize I don't know how they relate to our past. I wonder what memories they have or what they feel. Do they dwell on loss in private the way I do? How has our father's death shaped them? Have they grieved?

Sometimes I think it's indulgent to look back into the past. Instead of moving on, I stubbornly search for the broken pieces scattered behind our lives, trying to patch together a coherent story for myself.

But is a story actually required to live a life?

From my myopic view—because I live at a distance from them, because we love each other with unshakable conviction but also keep our inner lives separate, because I have my blind spots—I see that my siblings have forged ahead into the good lives held out to them: finding stable jobs, marrying Vietnamese partners, buying houses in the suburbs, and having children.

Unlike me, they have never expressed a desire to excavate our past. What's shattered is best left that way, they all seem to say in chorus.

Sometimes I wish I was more like them, living with no use for returns, physical or otherwise. A story of the past does nothing for them.

But I know that, even if they have no need for it now, the story is there, unspooling in the collection of images and in lurking memories. The past is still there, and our family is waiting to be examined.

I have four photographs not included in this archive. One day, I'd like to consider these photos with my siblings, to show them and ask questions, even though I know they might not see what I see or have the answers I'm looking for.

THE FIRST PHOTO I STOLE. I kept it safe in between the pages of a notebook, which I took all over Asia in a small backpack.

Someone is getting married, and my family poses for a portrait. In the image, my siblings are lined up in front of my parents. On the left, my second sister stands unsmiling in a gingham dress, one arm bent across her torso. She is caught off guard. My brother leans his head against her shoulder. He is in a T-shirt and green pants, rolled up at the hem. Next to him is my eldest sister, tallest of the bunch, in a ruffled dress with a bib collar, not looking directly at the camera. They are all wearing leather sandals, little toes peeking out; this detail reminds me that they too were once young—with childhoods not yet touched by the seeking of refuge.

Behind them, my mother is wearing a yellow áo dài, and my father is in a white button-up shirt. They are both thin, but my father is darker, burnt by the sun and seven years of hard labour in re-education camps. He is a political prisoner newly returned home.

On the wall behind them, in the top left corner, is the date "14.1.82" in red and the Chinese character for "double happiness" (囍). The repetition and symmetry, the two characters holding hands, is an auspicious symbol of completeness that hangs over the family. Nothing can go wrong if they stay together.

I first saw this photo when I was twenty-five. I was in Ho Chi Minh City by myself, a refugee returning as a foreigner to roam across its curved and scarred spine. I rode on the back of a motorbike to the house where my father's mother lived. She wasn't there, and when I went to the hospital to see her, I failed to pronounce her name properly. No one knew who I was looking for, so I walked the corridors, peeking into every room.

When I found her, my aunt was changing her diaper. The woman who had once carried my father inside her did not recognize me. I thought that seeing her would bring me closer to the father I didn't know. She was the most visceral proof that he existed.

I touched the weathered skin on her hand, and she opened her glassy eyes.

When I returned to the house later that day, my cousin welcomed me with open arms. She and I were born in the same year, and she is a more beautiful version of me, living the life I left behind. After she hugged me, I asked to see photo albums. It was the best way for us to catch up. She travelled up a flight of stairs and searched dusty cabinets to collect them for me. There were photos of weddings and funerals, vacations and return trips, pictures taken decades ago, and images captured abroad and then sent back here. Faces of aunts and uncles, relatives of relatives, and many strangers.

Then, sitting among these other people was my family. I pointed at the photo, and asked where it came from. My cousin said she didn't know, that she hardly ever looked at these albums. In a city trying to grow out of a war, no one has time for the past.

We have our own family albums in Canada, and they too sit untouched inside my mother's linen closet. There are a handful of photos with all six of us in them, often in the same tableau, with variations in clothing and age: mother and father behind two boys in between two girls. These photos were all taken at the same location—Turtle Lake in Ho Chi Minh City—years apart. In the albums, the photos sit next to other images, they belong to a longer narrative. They make sense because they don't have to bear the responsibility of telling the entire story of our lives. But what they do is hold the idea of a complete family, one that was brief and has since vanished.

I don't know how these photos made it across the Pacific. Did my mother smuggle them out of Vietnam? Did she have them when pirates—fishermen by day—pillaged our boat? Were they wrapped tight when we trekked through the jungle at night between borders? Were they with us as bombs went off around our camp? Who decided these photos were worth packing into our one big suitcase destined for Alberta? Or did they take a different route from ours? Were they rescued and carried over by an aunt or someone we knew?

When the Vietnam War ended, people burned their photos. Evidence of their past lives needed to disappear, and when more people fled the country in the following years, more photos were abandoned. I wonder why that lone family photo I saw in Vietnam was orphaned, left behind as the others migrated.

When my cousin left the room, I lifted the cellophane and slipped the photo into my pocket. Only the wall gecko saw what I did.

I returned to Canada and continued to carry the photo inside my notebook, where I kept a log of my travels, email addresses of people I met, and random notes. I wanted it close to me. I wanted this image to be my own story. Then one day I opened the book, and it was gone. I cried, thinking it might have slipped out at a random café or on the public bus, that it might be sitting in the trash somewhere or shredded to pieces. How did it travel so far only to get lost like this?

Years later, I was older and a little less sentimental. I lived in a different city, far from my mother, and on one of my return visits to Calgary I opened the family album. It's my way of catching up with time. As I flipped through the pages, five familiar faces looked back at me.

Someone had taken the photo from my notebook and returned it to its proper place, released it from being hostage to my nostalgia.

It's my favourite family photo because I'm not in it. It makes me happy to know that there was a family before I came into this world, that a family is possible without me. It means we can still be a family even if one of us is missing.

But I'm not being completely truthful. I *am* there in the photo; you just can't see me. I'm inside my mother, growing, waiting to join them, to wear a pair of leather sandals too. And one day, I will grow up and come back to steal this captured moment.

THE SECOND PHOTO IS MY immigration photo. There are two copies. I have one, and the other is locked up in a government cabinet or vault somewhere, collecting dust. I'm standing in front of a wooden door with metal hinges. I'm not smiling; as with passport photos, I was told to keep still, hold my breath.

This was supposed to be a happy moment, the beginning of something more than the little boy in the picture could ever imagine possible. What this photo doesn't reveal are the three years I waited in a series of Thai refugee camps for my new life to begin.

The first camp was a makeshift open barracks. Each family had a bed, and we all shared a large latrine. This camp was the worst, not because of the living conditions, but because of the guards. The refugee men they would haul into fields at all hours of the day, make them strip and exercise to exhaustion before a beating. The refugee women they would come for when it was dark. My teenaged sisters never slept through the night; they'd be woken up and moved to different beds by my mother, seeking trustworthy men to protect them. She would smother their faces with mud, disguising their young beauty.

The second camp was a complex of thatched-roof houses. I had my seventh birthday celebration in one of them. There's a photo of me behind a table displaying bounty—spring rolls, noodles, a box of raisins, and a radio. All these luxuries were procured by my mother through the saving and bartering of UN rations. We'd recently learned, through a letter, that my father had lost patience and got on a boat to join us. For months there had been no word from him—captured, drowned, imprisoned, executed? He was just gone. All this I heard through whispers and tears shed when everyone was supposed to be asleep.

I'm not smiling in the photo. I will never want another birthday party. I will tell my friends I prefer something quiet and low-key.

For my present, I received a brand new pair of Bata running shoes—to be used in the event of a bomb raid and our flight into the surrounding jungle.

The third camp we stayed in was a processing centre. We had our own private living quarters, supported by a wooden frame and thin plaster walls. Outside, there were large trees that children climbed to collect fruit. There were fields for running with abandon, long dusty roads, and sun that lasted forever. There was a commissary that sold all kinds of practical and novel items, like clothes, rice, and soap, to those who could afford them. This was where I tasted my first M&M—the sugar coating melting on my tongue before the depth of chocolate activated a feeling I still have no language for. There was an open-air movie theatre, where I saw my first porno when the wrong reel was projected. White flesh upon flesh. In those few seconds my body recognized it wanted more of those taut muscles, the length of a man.

None of these refugee camps exist anymore, but people have kept their memory alive with online memorials of photographs and stories.

My immigration photo does not belong to this collective archive. It doesn't even belong to me. It's attached to a piece of paper with a staple. And at the bottom of the page is a warning: "This document is the property of the government of Canada." A circular stamp with the designation *Canadian Embassy–Immigration–Ambassade du Canada* catches a corner of the photo, imprinting itself as a curve over my chest. This was the photo that allowed me to get on a plane with my family and arrive in Calgary during the coldest winter month. It's the first photo in a series of photos that will allow me to move freely across the world and be welcomed back "home" by customs officers in Canada.

Yet this photo is not a portrait of freedom but of capture, weighed down by the official black ink, the legalese, and the sharp metal that binds it to the immigration form.

This photo says I am a "Citizen of—STATELESS." But it also gave me a number, and that number gave me rights.

I'm supposed to be grateful for everything this immigration photo has given me, but I don't remember the day it was taken, and I don't know that boy—posing alone, without family—even though he looks like me. I keep this photo safe in my possession because if there's one thing I know for sure, it's that everything can be taken away.

• • •

THE THIRD PHOTOGRAPH WAS PUBLISHED in the *Los Angeles Times*. I found it in the Southeast Asian Archive in Irvine, California. I'd been sitting there for less than an hour, and I was holding a news clipping from a brown folder that contained an image of my mother.

The discoloured newsprint between my fingers felt so thin, like it might disintegrate, or it might not even be real. I focused my eyes to see the grainy image.

She is the only one in the frame returning the camera's gaze, looking straight into the lens, as if anticipating the future moment in which I would witness her presence in our past. The smile on her face is conspiratorial, giving me permission to keep looking.

But I didn't.

I lifted my head and watched the co-op student standing in socks and sandals making copies at the machine, his outline lit up at intervals. The archivist was absorbed in a pile of files. She was trying to figure out what to do with them or where they should belong. One pile became two, became three. A beam of sunlight filtered through the large window, the clock on the wall said it was still morning.

The night before, I had lain awake in a motel room by the freeway and thought about people discovering family documents in the archives. As the red light of the alarm clock flashed *0:00, 0:00* into the darkness, I entertained the distant possibility that I too might stumble upon a small trace of myself. But when the moment actually happened, all I could feel was the uncanny suspension of the haunted present and a strange sense of desperation. Time was running out, and a block of ice was melting inside my stomach.

I looked again to make sure it was her face and not someone else's.

I couldn't trust myself—is that really my mother?

Then I read the caption underneath the photo: "Vietnamese 'boat people' in an English class at the Phanat Nikhom camp in Thailand. Tuesday, December 20, 1988." It *was* her, confirmed by time and circumstance. The years that had passed—and the forgetting that had settled in between their cracks—are punctured by the image of my mother staring into a camera.

And there I was, twenty-five years later, meeting her stare.

Many eyes had seen this photo before me. But what did this photo reveal to readers of a national newspaper as they drank morning coffee and flipped through its pages?

My mother seems happy, sitting cross-legged on the floor with other refugees, who grasp their notebooks and pens, eager to absorb the lesson. The teacher, a missionary, is giving them the words to be traded for a job, a house, an extended hand. The ability to one day read this write-up about their lives.

What you're supposed to see in this photo is hope, refugees in transition, in the process of becoming American residents. A success story.

But when I look at this photo, what I see is the mundane moments of our lives embedded in a historical record. What we went through really happened. Another self once existed, and might still be living within us. As distant as the past is, we can travel back there too, not just in memory, but through a physical photograph.

What I see is my mother, who is still here, who took us across the world and spent every day making sure we stayed alive.

Someone called out her name, she looked up into the camera, there was a moment of recognition—decades later, on the other side of that photo, was me.

That night, from my motel room, I called my mother long-distance, reaching her in a house buried by snow. I told her that I'd found a photograph of her. She wanted to see, so I emailed it to my sister, who opened the file and showed her the image. She laughed, and couldn't believe it.

She asked whether I'd eaten. It's her way of telling me that she loves me.

For the next few minutes, we chatted about the weather, everyone's health, and the food she'd been cooking.

We circled back to the photo and she laughed again, telling me she did not recognize herself: that young, thin refugee from the past. Her memory no longer held that woman.

THE FOURTH PHOTO SITS IN a frame on the wall, displayed for all to see.

It's of me and my father. When visitors ask, I tell them it's the only photo that exists of just the two of us. I'm sitting on his lap, and he is laughing so hard his head is thrown back, his mouth open, and you can see all his teeth. His left arm is holding me tight, pulling me into him. My smile is more coy, more contained than his laugh, as I look straight into the camera. I'm wearing shorts, and my bare legs dangle above the ground, one sandal about to slip off.

I should say that the photo sat in a frame, in the past tense. The photo no longer exists. It burned in a house fire, and I don't have another copy.

I can't remember exactly what the photo looks like. I no longer recall the precise details. Every time I think about it, I see a different image. I can't recall what my father was wearing—a chemise? a T-shirt?—or where it was taken—at our house? a garden?—or the shape of his pose—hunched? upright? I don't recall his face. Was I the one sitting in a chair? Was it me who was laughing? Was my father urging me to look at the camera?

Let me try to remember.

He wasn't laughing or smiling at all.

Let me try again.

Are my arms around him? Or are his arms around me?

Try again.

I'm alone in the photo.

He's not there.

It's actually a photo of him leaning against a wall, arms crossed. He is wearing a pair of brown leather sandals, dark-grey trousers, and a white button-up shirt. He is smiling for the camera, but everything about the image is enveloped in sadness.

What I'm telling you is not a lie. This is just how memory works. The most useful thing about remembering is that you can make it up. The photo of me and my father no longer exists or never existed, except in memory and here on this page.

5

ON THE BACK OF A TIGER

IN THE FALL OF 2020, I'm asked to give a public lecture. The organizer wants me to talk about storytelling. I have the option to do the lecture virtually or to wait until in-person events start up again. Longing for human interaction, I opt for the latter, hopeful that someday soon I can sit in a room with others.

The organizer, a very nice and well-meaning woman, then asks if I could bring my mother to give "testimony" to her refugee experience. Doing so, she reasons, would add a "punch of reality," a body of evidence to my expertise.

I imagine my mother with her broken English and dignified grace—dressed in her blue chiffon blouse and pinstripe jacket, looking better than anyone in the room—speaking into a lowered microphone, telling the audience all about her secret pain and unspeakable trauma. They would part their lips and lean forward. Some people would shake their heads and turn to their neighbour in shock and compassion, all the while looking past the woman in front of them. What they are after is a confession of things they already know about refugees. The same old story.

I politely decline, telling the organizer that my mother is a private person.

I THINK ABOUT THE CHASM between how others want refugees, like my family, to tell stories and the way refugees actually talk—a bit cautious, a bit dissociated—and what we talk about.

Once, when I was a teenager, my family squeezed into a white van and drove along Highway 1. The Rocky Mountains rose dramatically in front of us; their magnificent scale making the vehicles crawling along the road look like tiny insects.

Getting on the road again after a quick rest stop, my eldest sister asked, "Wasn't she singing when it happened?"

"The singing quickly became screaming," my second sister responded.

My mother imitated the woman in a high-pitched voice, *"Help me please, I'm dying, I'm dying!"*

"Terrible," my brother-in-law, in front of the wheel, chimed in.

"So terrible," the women all emphasized at the same time.

"How did she get out, again?" my eldest sister asked.

My mother responded, as if chastising her for forgetting, "Remember, that little boy, Thi, remember him? He heard her and ran to get his older brother."

"A bamboo pole, right, Má?"

"Yes. And three grown men."

"She stank for weeks," my second sister added.

Our entire family erupted into laughter, shaking the van from side to side.

"No one in the camp wanted to come near her," my mother said.

"She tried everything to get the smell out," my second sister said.

"Can you imagine? A pit that everyone used—" my eldest sister said.

"—in the heat." My mother scrunched her face.

The van shook again, and the other drivers on their way to the mountains for the long weekend saw us swerving like a drunk.

My second sister interrupted the laughter and stuck her hands out flat. "Those planks. They were just this big."

"And rotting too. It could've been any one of us!"

My eldest sister remembered, "Ah, it was tomato sauce!"

"Yes, she had to soak in a tub of that—"

"—and boiled lime peels," my mother completed the memory.

"Still stank after, though," my brother said, joining the story for the first time.

We burst out in laughter again.

My mother slapped her hands together in joyful abandon.

• • •

As I RECALL THIS MEMORY of us recalling a memory, I'm struck by how our stories emerge at odd, unexpected moments. For years, we would not talk about what we went through, each of us maintaining our own private understanding of events, and then all it took was what my sister called a "disgusting" rest-stop bathroom for this story of an unfortunate woman, whose meagre weight buckled one of the rotting planks inside an outhouse to surface. A chorus of voices, each adding a detail, driving the story along to its tragicomic conclusion.

I wonder if, and when, the woman tells this story now. And whether she can laugh at the past too.

We were on our way to Banff National Park. The white van was packed with camping tents, coolers with steaks and jumbo tiger shrimp, a propane tank, and, most importantly, a rice cooker.

Summer camping became a new family tradition after our arrival in Canada. The majestic Rockies, with tops still capped in snow, the towering evergreens as a canopy, the night sky with a million visible stars, made us feel as though we could escape our everyday life for a few days. But my mother, with a portable stove, still made sure we ate well, making stir-fries and grilling marinated meats. The quality of food remained the same, as if she had a full kitchen in the wilderness. Camping made us feel less like outsiders who had to learn every custom in a new country. Living among trees and sleeping on the ground, doing everything makeshift, was something we knew how to do.

But every year, without fail, there were bear warnings. We weren't the only ones who wanted to eat well. Bears would come out at night looking for food left in the open. The year before this trip, a hungry grizzly ripped through a tent where a family of three slept. When the father woke and, in shock, tried to shoo it away, the bear mauled him as his wife and child watched in silent terror.

My mother was completely risk-averse, avoiding any semblance of danger because she's seen so much of it in her life already. She never learned to drive a car in Canada for fear of dying in an accident. She washed every leaf of lettuce three times, once with vinegar, once with salt, and once with water, lest some speck of dirt and, with it, illness entered our bodies. She always reminded us of what awaited when we left the house: black ice, falling debris, the wind that brought cold, a man with a knife.

And yet, even when she heard news of the murderous bear, we continued camping every summer. Fear never deterred us. Sleeping in tents outdoors, I think, overwrote our experience of what *camp* could mean. Camping in the Canadian wilderness reminded us of the time we spent in the refugee camps, but it also transformed that experience from one of uncertainty and anxiety into one of our own wilful making. We had fun trying to stay alive. We didn't know that we also needed this revised meaning to survive the many years to come.

• • •

DURING A CONVERSATION WITH MY mother many years removed from the camping trips that happened less and less frequently until they stopped altogether, I asked her about the decision to escape Vietnam. She said that she hadn't known—couldn't have known—what would happen. Making a decision in postwar Vietnam was a gamble. Deciding was like having one's hands zip-tied at the back before being shoved into the night jungle, the muzzle of a rifle prodding one's back.

What was a decision, anyway?

"We were riding on the back of a tiger," she said.

To ride on the back of a tiger means to accept the risk of certain death. Or, more precisely, to see its eyes glowing in the bush, through the dark foliage, and to step into the tangled jungle anyway.

THIS IS THE STORY MY mother told me when, as an adult, I finally had the courage to ask:

Your father and I tuned the radio to the perfect volume, loud enough so we could listen to the BBC and Voice of America report on rising compassion fatigue for Vietnamese boat people, who were arriving daily on the shores of Malaysia, Indonesia, and the Philippines, but low enough not to wake you and your siblings. All the refugee camps, we heard, were going to be shut down.

"What now," we whispered to each other. "What now?"

The application to reunite with my parents in Canada had been rejected. The officials considered us a separate family that didn't need reunifying. Another application to go to the United States languished in bureaucratic red tape. The letters we wrote received no response.

To answer our own question of what now, we went to see a fortune teller—not once but twice. The first time, we took you and your siblings with us. The fortune teller, an old man with a mole growing on his cheek, told us that everyone could cross the border and get on a boat—except your father. A dark cloud hung over him, the fortune teller said. He had a vision that only five bodies walked through the shining doors of an airport.

He said: "Do not go."

We asked him to chart everyone's paths on yellow pieces of paper, then paid the man and left.

At home, your father said, "That man speaks nonsense. Don't believe a single word."

I said, "Yes."

The next week, we went, just the two of us, to see a different fortune teller, someone who would speak sense, who would divine a different future, one that would reflect the only present we had. We needed someone to say, "Yes, yes, you can go. Go now!"

What we needed was not a prediction but a confirmation.

The second fortune teller was younger than the first. His glasses were thick like a windowpane. He told us there would be some difficulties, but we would overcome it all.

Your father and I sighed with relief. Our grip on each other's hand slackened.

The fortune teller went on to predict a prosperous new life filled with many dollar bills, successful careers, and a gardened house in America, before pausing to take a closer look at the diagrams he'd drawn up. Wait. Something didn't add up; something had gone wrong; he took back all the bills, careers, and houses, rewinding time because of some miscalculation on a birth date.

His new verdict: "Do not go. It won't end well."

He said he saw only five figures sitting inside a boat at night, its side crashing against the raging sea.

A tiger roared.

I BEGAN TO SEE THAT to ride on the back of a tiger is to tempt fate—to will another outcome into being in the face of an undesirable one. To believe in the possibility of the impossible. Hope in the blinding dark.

THIS IS THE STORY I created from memory when I finally had the courage to remember:

Knees to chest, back against back. Hands gripping feet. Elbows wedged into crevices left open between bodies, poking thighs or ribs or chests. That was how we sat inside a boat four or five metres long, sailing out of Kampong Som bay in Cambodia toward the coast of Thailand. The feel of someone else's breath on our faces reminded us that we were still alive.

Sight was not the primary sense here, because everything occurred in the dark. No flashlights, no moon. We couldn't see because we had to remain invisible, unseen by police, pirates, or vengeful spirits. The engine sputtering awake marked the beginning of our journey. Waves lapping against the side of the boat. As our pupils adjusted to the lack of light, we made out the round heads in front of us, still figures beneath a mottled sky, lives given over to what was already written in the ancient stars.

The sea entered our noses as molecules of salt, scratching at the back of dry mouths. Our thirst was electric, tricking us into believing we might never drink fresh water again. Our groaning stomachs drowned out by the churning of sea water. Our shivering limbs turned prickly like goose skin as the boat picked up speed, the air and water pulsing at our bodies, whipping our hair everywhere.

And then the smell of diesel began filling our lungs, leaving a bitter taste on our tongues, making us light-headed. We were lulled by the sea's rocking motion. When we noticed water reaching our calves, it took a few moments to realize we were starting to sink. We used any vessel we could—a can, a shoe—to scoop out the water, which slowed down our sinking, keeping the water surface just below the boat's gunwale. And then, when desperation hit, we used our cupped hands.

To ride on the back of a tiger is to step foot inside a boat without knowing how to swim.

ONCE, SOMEONE TOLD ME A story. I don't remember who it was, but that doesn't really matter now. After they finished, I saw through a watery screen—black stripes shimmering on orange fur, the ferocious face of a tiger ready to pounce on unsuspecting prey.

This is what I made out:

When the Communists advanced southward in April 1975, my father, a military police captain soon to be major, was stationed in the coastal city of Nha Trang. He and his men gathered in a warehouse to decide what they should do as the nation they defended began collapsing. After twenty minutes of deliberation, my father led them to the port and used his AK-47 to force two fleeing ships to take everyone to Saigon, the last South Vietnamese stronghold. There, smaller boats were waiting to take these men to American ships anchored out in the open waters. These ships would transport them to a military base in Guam, from where they'd be flown directly to the United States.

As the men boarded the final boat, one of them asked my father to take a seat and join them. My father stood there for a moment, looked out at the horizon, and thought of his wife, children, and mother. Then he placed a firm hand on the young man's shoulder, "Go, I'll take the next one," he said. A familiar reassuring grin on his face, a look they were all used to.

What would happen next was unknown to him.

A tiger roars.

6

AN ACUTE ACCENT

A MONTH AFTER THE WOMAN next door fell off the balcony, I start
my online Spanish class.

The city is under lockdown, and the number of Covid cases
continues to rise. The new year begins on a quiet note, but the
one that had just passed was a year of death. Every headline
was a devastating number, abstracting the magnitude of lives
lost. Every crack in our personal lives, society, and the world
exposed and amplified.

Not knowing how to regain control of life, I decide to learn
a new language.

From my desk next to the window, I can look down nine
floors and see where her body lay that evening. In its place

now are dead flowers and burnt candle holders, left there by well-meaning strangers. But every time I lift my head, I see the body's outline underneath the orange tarp; my eyes always find the exact spot. I'm compelled to look again and again, recalling how I glimpsed a hand in a pool of dark blood when a cop came by with his flashlight.

But it feels rude to be learning a new language in the wake of this death. I don't know who she was and have no idea how or why she fell, but I haven't been able to sleep undisturbed or walk through my living room without feeling a chill brush the back of my neck.

"Hola!" a voice calls out from the screen. "Can you hear me?"

My instructor is an older man, originally from Central America, with a calm demeanour and large glasses. Some people wave their hands while others say yes into their microphones. He asks us why we're taking this course. My classmates list their reasons—travel, retirement, Spanish-speaking lovers—and I begin to panic. I guide my cursor over to the Leave Meeting button. I could blame it on bad internet connection or malfunctioning Zoom. The last thing I want right now is to introduce myself to strangers, talk into the machine in front of me. This moment becomes gratuitous, a bit too much—being alive is stupid. I cannot understand why I have this body that continues to breathe, to make sounds and sit here now. If it's so easy to die—just lean over and fall off a ledge—then why live?

I hear my name called. I'm flustered, but I manage to unmute myself.

· · ·

THE BODY LAY ON THE pavement for four hours.

Yellow police tape separated it from the living, who skirted the perimeter with curiosity. In the building opposite mine, anonymous silhouettes on balconies peered down at the scene, asking questions about the body that remained there in the cold, alone.

This is what death looks like.

I realized that I'd never seen a dead body—and this struck me because I'd been living with death for the past twelve months, learning how to grieve Don's sudden passing, and in turn my father's death decades ago.

Every night, death followed me underneath the covers. It greeted me in the morning with dry toast, and then stubbornly shadowed my daily movements—but I'd never been so physically close to a dead body, never seen it so crudely.

Seeing the woman's body made me want to touch Don, to feel the texture of his skin and the warmth of blood coursing through him. I wanted to have one last meeting so I could plead with him to stay alive. But I never got to hug his body and say goodbye. This is what bothers me most. This is the worst part of it all. One moment he was breathing, and the next he was gone. His organs taken out and rearranged into other bodies.

It was the same with my father. There was no farewell, no time to prepare or come to terms, no chance to bargain. I was in a refugee camp, and he was somewhere else, making his way toward me and my family. One day he was in this world, and the next he was not.

I don't know what happened to my father's body. There's only a void in the shape of a man, and inside that void are stray questions and floating what-ifs. My father's missing body has multiplied into an endless story with no direction, stumbling toward an inconclusion.

Without a body, mourning is complicated. Magical thinking kicks in, and a splinter of doubt lodges itself in my mind— but, but, he *could* show up one day. Out of the blue, he could finally arrive, find us, and we would become a whole family again. There is no certainty that he's *really* dead. No incontrovertible evidence. No body to appease stubborn logic.

But—

But still, I must grieve. Must go through the motions of grieving.

Psychologists call what I experience *unresolved grief*, where the duration of bereavement is extended, resulting in a range of pathological symptoms: melancholia, anger, obsession, isolation. But what does it mean for grief to be resolved? Didn't Freud say that the standard course of healthy mourning involves consuming the lost object, incorporating it into the ego so it remains forever part of the self?

Buddhists in Vietnam believe that the dead body must be cleansed for safe passage into the afterlife. One tradition calls for digging up the grave and reopening the coffin after three years of burial. The decomposed remains, mostly bones, are then cleaned and transferred to a new resting place. The body requires earthly attention for its transcendental transitions. And mourning does not expire: the designated period of mourning often lasts for years, and the dead can never be forgotten; they find a place on the family altar, invoked every time a stick of incense is burned, celebrated on every death anniversary.

The dead, then, always surround the living. But the soul of an unattended-to body roams outside the cycle of reincarnation. There are no chants, no meals, no coin in the mouth to help it move along.

Without the rituals done for a body, does my father remain trapped in this world?

Don's heart is keeping another body alive.

The woman's body dropped into my life when I had experienced two deaths and no body. Her death is hers and hers alone; but it bled into my grief that night, and she will forever remain in my story.

I DECIDE TO TAKE A walk to catch the brief afternoon light. In the park, with its patches of dirty, melting snow, women are pushing strollers. A dog barks. A toddler lags behind. The sun strikes through bare branches to land on tents, a whole city of tents with people seeking shelter.

—and suddenly I see my partner, slumped at his desk. His head is down, eyes closed, arms hanging loose, unresponsive.

I break into a run, heading toward home. Brown slush splashes all over my sneakers and jeans. I'm panting when I

VINH NGUYEN

enter the building, forgetting to put on my mask. As I exit the elevator, I bump into the building's custodian. Her cleaning cart stands between me and my door.

"Did you know what happen?" she asks, pointing at my neighbour's apartment, which has a small police seal over its threshold.

"No," I say absent-mindedly, wanting to get past her and to my partner.

She gestures with her hand for me to come closer, and I lean in. She whispers, and with her thick Spanish accent under a mask, I can barely make out her words. "A friend visiting."

She folds her body, as if looking over a ledge. "Accident."

"So very sad." She shrugs.

I nod my head in agreement and squeeze by.

When I finally open the door, my partner calls out, "How was your walk?"

I let out the long breath I didn't know I was holding.

I DO THE INADEQUATE CALCULATIONS in my head. If I go back to Calgary once a year during the Christmas holidays and she visits me in Toronto every summer, I'll get to see my mother perhaps twenty times. Twenty-five, thirty times if I'm more diligent, if she lives well into her eighties. But factor in contingencies like the pandemic and the busyness of life or the unpredictability of death, I'd have to realistically subtract five to ten years, this a conservative estimate. So perhaps I might have ten or fifteen opportunities to see my mother again, to be in her physical presence and touch her breathing body.

I hold up both hands and count my ten fingers. They look grotesque. I've never been good at math. I can't be sure if this is the best-case or worst-case scenario. Am I a fortunate person or am I cursed?

My vision is cloudy—lost in the fog of grief.

On my last trip before the pandemic shut down air travel, my friend J and her partner took me on a hike up to the Griffith Observatory. When we reached the top, the view of sprawling downtown Los Angeles was stunning. The expansive beauty and the tender orange light as the late afternoon sun began moving westward brought tears to my eyes. I felt the most immense exhaustion, my body both hollow and filled with the heaviest of metals. I couldn't go on walking, so I slowly fell back from my friends, stopping at a small spot under a tree.

Then, from behind, J said to me, "Perhaps it's a gift."

"What?" I turned around.

"Don's passing is preparing you for what's to come."

I stood still.

My friend wrapped her small arms around my chest. "Everything will be easier from now on."

I've thought about this moment often, about the great wisdom in J's words. At that time, I was looking for meaning in death. I wanted it to have some kind of purpose, or else it would be senseless. And if it were senseless, then my suffering would be useless. Nothing about existing would matter the way I needed it to.

So what my friend did was open up a road map for me. Don's death led me to my father's death, which will lead me to the most devastating death of all: my mother's. When it comes, along this inevitable but horrifying path, I will be battle-tested, will know what to do, will be calloused against its power.

Another friend, who lost one parent as a child and the other parent as an adult, once told me that losing both felt like being violently cast out into the world without a compass. The last lifeline severed. You're left turning corners in the dark, she said, and when you think you've found your way, you realize there's no one like you. Those who made you, who held the keys to your story, are forever gone. Having siblings or children, she said, wasn't the same.

When my father died, I had my mother to break my fall. Her body was a place for me to land. Her cradle of sinew and bone, fat and organ, tissue and nerve absorbed the worst of the impact.

But who can buffer my plummet when she is gone?

My friend J is correct. A death is a gift because it forces us to open our eyes to what we know but must intentionally forget in order to continue living our lives. It makes us less naive—to see that death is always on its way. Creeping toward our security while we remain tediously unaware.

But my mother's forthcoming death, the one I know is getting closer and closer, but will still—must—stubbornly shove to the sidelines of my consciousness, will not be easier because of the deaths that came before. Learning to grieve Don and my father is not preparing me for the loss of my mother. What it's doing is providing me with a warning: be vigilant, don't look away, it's nearing.

You will be destroyed.

Know that.

I GATHERED WITH FRIENDS TO celebrate a birthday. It was a biting cold night, and we all shared tough pizzas that came out of a stone oven. A, whose birthday it was, had recently suffered a miscarriage. She teared up when someone asked how she was doing. Her husband, C, put his hand on her back. We all forced smiles onto our faces when she said she was okay. I thought about what it must be like to carry life inside one's body, but also to hold death, a mass of flesh and tissue that once had a heartbeat. That would have had a name. It was possible for death to exist inside one's body too, and to experience its extrication.

Another friend, S, arrived late. He came in, hugged everyone, and sat across from D, who had been his lover for over a decade. They'd parted ways not too long before. They were cordial and tender toward each other, but in between them, stretched out across the fourteen inches of pizza, was the death of a potential life together, children, a house, compromises, old age. Everything that was and could have been. Loss was materialized in your ex sitting in a chair, picking a piece of olive off a slice. This loss you can hug, and ask if they've seen friends you once visited together.

My partner kissed me gently on the cheek, and all I wanted was for Don not to be gone forever, to see my father one last time, or to have a funeral with an open casket.

At some point, I said to S that I was scared of death, that it had suddenly become real. I felt weak and blindsided. That I, out of anyone, should have been more prepared, should have seen it coming. I thought that I knew death and defined myself through it, having read about it in books, written about it in essays, heard about it through others' experiences. And, of course, there was my own father. But I felt dumb now, requiring an actual death to realize that death was real after all these years. I wondered if growing old was just experiencing the things one already knows.

When my partner and I walked home, we passed a group of young hipsters without jackets huddled outside a dive bar, red-faced, smoking a joint. They had so much experience ahead of them, and from that moment on, the people in my life would die one by one, and there was nothing I could do about it.

DURING A LATER SPANISH LESSON, we learn to count numbers. *Uno, dos, tres.* When we get into the double digits, I lose track. For some reason, my mind can't follow them and their replication, even when they are written out in words. All the infinite combinations and possibilities, the unceasingness of it, overwhelms the moment.

Frustrated, I look up from the screen and notice that the light of dusk lingers. Only a week ago, at this time, it was completely dark outside. The days are getting longer now. I see the spot where the body was, and nothing has changed.

I think about the morning after the woman fell off the balcony. The entire courtyard was cleaned, returned to normal, the police tape removed and the blood washed away, as if the body had never been there. A few people stood around watching their dogs sniff each other's behinds. One little terrier came by and licked the spot, circled around and wagged its tail. Then, finding nothing of interest, it moved on to the green turf and did its business. The owner dutifully prepared a plastic bag and scooped the shit up in his hand.

Next to me, on a bench by the window, the potted coleus plant reaches its stems of green-and-pink leaves toward the dying light. On two tips, small white-and-blue flowers grow in a spike. The flowers bloom because the plant knows the end is near. This is its attempt to reproduce itself before it shrivels and recedes from the world.

In soil, the fallen buds would take hold, turn sun and water into life. But here they lie on the linoleum floor, drying up before I run a rude vacuum over them.

· · ·

THE MONTHS PASS AND THERE is more light. The sun makes more frequent appearances and stays with the day for hours on end. On one of our walks, my partner points out the depth of new green, so crisp and lucent, growing on the trees in our neighbourhood. It's something he's never noticed before.

A collective hope arrives in the form of a vaccine, and like many collective hopes, it reveals itself to be reserved for only a few. I am one of these few, because I've migrated to a corner of the globe we call the First World. I get to prolong my life.

The day I receive the second shot, I go online and book a flight to Calgary. I call my mother and tell her I'm returning to the house. She's happy, and tells me she will cook all the foods I've craved but couldn't eat in the two years we've not seen each other.

When I hang up, I wonder again if I'm fortunate or cursed. How to even begin? I start to re-tally the number of years in my head, trying not to overestimate or ask for too much from life.

One, two, three . . .

7

WAITING

EVEN THOUGH I'M FLYING DOMESTIC, I arrive at Toronto's Pearson International Airport many hours in advance. I don't want to miss this flight to Calgary, this long-awaited journey back to my mother.

So I sit in the mostly empty waiting lounge by the gate, holding my ID tight and my backpack close to me.

A family of six appears to float down the moving walkway toward my gate. When they disembark, I see they are all wearing padded coats, not suitable for the hot and dry Calgary summer. They are pulling new suitcases and carrying plastic bags, but the eldest son, around fifteen, has a blue International

Organization for Migration (IOM) tote hanging on his left shoulder.

It's clear that this family has come a long way, and Calgary might not even be their final destination.

They settle at a spot with seats facing one another, their bodies forming an imperfect circle. I watch as the mother, as if by magic, produces four cheeseburgers from her bag. She unwraps each one and hands them over to her children. They are hungry, but they eat their prizes with delicacy, savouring each bite.

As the lounge begins to fill up, no one takes a seat near them. But they don't seem to notice or mind, speaking loudly in their language and moving about with unrestrained ease. When the mother notices that her youngest son has a yellow food stain on his shirt, she takes out a handkerchief, wets it with saliva, and begins rubbing at the spot vigorously.

I feel how far I am from them. I look at my phone and see a message from my mother.

"Bring a hat."

WHEN I CAME OUT TO my mother in 2011, she said, "It's okay. You're normal. There're lots of people like you." She said the word *normal* in English.

I waited until the last moment of my visit to Calgary, right before I had to leave for the airport, to tell her. I'd waited thirty years. All that waiting spilled out of me as tears, and when they came, they could not be contained. I sat on the kitchen stool and sobbed.

She was preparing lunch, noodle soup for me to eat before I got on the plane. She had been moving through another ordinary morning before I barged into the kitchen and said, "Mom, I have something to tell you . . . I'm gay."

I dropped it on the floor, and it lay there like a cracked egg—the yolk broken and oozing, the shell in fragments.

My mother put her knife down, leaving the cilantro half-chopped, its bittersweet scent filling the room. Steam escaped from the boiling pot behind her, but she remained calm and turned the dial to switch off the stove.

I was shaking. I had been rehearsing what I would say over and over again since dawn, walking up and down the stairs, opening and closing doors. I had a plan. If she reacted badly, I would yell at her, accuse her of never knowing me. I'd storm out and flee on the plane, and there would be thousands of miles as a buffer between me and my disappointment.

I was worried about protecting myself, not about protecting her. But she didn't need protecting. She had seen all that life could do to a person, so her son coming out was never going to shatter the refuge she had worked so hard to build for her children.

She led me to the couch and told me what she knew I needed to hear.

"I understand." Her face stoic.

And then, "Nothing will change."

All I could muster in response was a silent nod.

"My child."

Seeing my mother's tender resolve made me cry even more. It made me realize how much I still needed her to be my mother. I could describe coming out as release and freedom, but for me that afternoon it was a longing to come home, to be my mother's son all over again.

Seeing my tears, my mother thought I was ashamed and conflicted.

"The most important thing is to be a person with integrity—to respect yourself," she said.

What for me was relief, she saw as shame. But relief is sometimes just shame taking its final gasp, asphyxiated from the inside out.

She put a hand on my shoulder and said, "Mẹ thương con." *Mother loves child, I love you.*

I couldn't stop crying. All I wanted in that moment was to unpack my suitcase and stay with her forever.

Later, she insisted on going with me to the airport. We sat in the car in silence as my sister drove along the endless Calgary highways, the flat prairies around us broken only by intersections and clusters of suburban houses. I thought about how many times we would have to say goodbye to each other in the years to come.

At the airport, she gave me a hug. My arms tried to memorize the impression of her tiny body, the feel of warmth as her head pressed against my torso. Then she placed her hand on the small of my back and steered me through the throng of people, away from her.

On the plane, I started crying again as the flight attendants performed the safety demonstration. The woman next to me stared straight ahead and casually slipped on her earphones. I peered out the window and watched the runway outside, a moving puzzle of trucks, planes, and small people in neon-orange vests. Then the world picked up speed and began to blur. It tilted as I was lifted into the air and the ground that had held me just seconds before dropped beneath me.

I closed the shade and shut my eyes, as if for the first time.

MY MOTHER IS THE SECOND child and eldest daughter in a family of fifteen. She was born in the late 1940s in an occupied nation trying to fight its way out of colonial rule and into self-determination. The Vietnam into which she was born was already at war. Everything that marked her passage through life—accords and escalations, coups and offensives, counter-insurgencies and curfews—occurred under violence.

When the war was over, there was nothing left: a country in ruins, millions of people dead, an imprisoned husband, young children to raise, and no way to make a living. In 1975, when the fighting ended, my mother was a high school teacher. My father was a captain in the fallen Army of the Republic of

Vietnam. This army and the nation it defended only exist now in a yellow heritage flag with three red horizontal stripes—representing the blood of its people—and memories scattered across the diaspora.

The exception of war was ordinary life for my mother, and she waited for peace, only to discover it came in the form of tanks rolling down a boulevard. Peace was a termination slip from the school and an official letter inviting her husband to a brief meeting. That meeting turned into seven years of incarceration in re-education camps. After waiting for so long, she realized there were more battles to be fought. A new war—which was only the old one hobbling forward on crutches—became ordinary life again.

But now it took shape as three hungry mouths to feed. Her children, my siblings, needed both a mother and a father, so she stepped into the city's battered streets and spent her days squatting curbside by an open suitcase containing loose cigarettes and a lighter. Whether the family ate depended on how many men had enough money to satisfy their nicotine craving. When she realized cigarettes were small game, she began trafficking in gold, the most precious and stable material in a black market. She learned to hustle in the toughest of economies, befriending gangsters, evading cops, and getting out of deals gone wrong.

When I came out to her, she had long left this past behind. She had escaped Vietnam and spent her life in Canada, cooking at home and tending to her garden. But to get there, she had to carry her children on a boat and through the jungles, then survive years in refugee camps. She had to find her way to a new country and build a different life for her broken family.

And she did all this without her husband.

For a long time, she waited to hear from him, knowing in her exhausted bones that he'd met the fate of many other refugees in the open water.

She waits no more. Time belongs to her now.

Time, minutes and hours and days and years slowly dripping from a kitchen tap, is what my mother has in abundance. Time is her reward for living when others died. Living is not a resolution to war, but its long-lasting residue.

A COUPLE WEEKS AFTER I came out, my mother called to check up on me in Toronto. She wanted to learn more and ask questions.

Was I sure?

"Of course I'm sure."

Might it have been a bad fever I had when I was a child?

"That's not how people become gay."

Might it have been the influence of friends?

"Yes, but not in the way you think."

Could this be something that I reconsider because the world is so unforgiving?

"No, Mom, I cannot."

"If this is the case, then you must take every precaution," she replied. Make yourself smaller so the surface that can be attacked and injured is minimized.

If there's one thing she knows for certain, it's that anything can happen at any moment. You can wake up one morning and lose everything. When this happens, nothing can save you, not even your mother. If you are not vigilant, then life will slip out of your hands, and all of it, the suffering, the waiting, the effort, will have been a waste.

SHE CALLED AGAIN THE NEXT week because the face of Jun Lin, the Chinese international student Luka Magnotta murdered, was plastered all over the news. She asked if I had read the horrific news, if I'd seen what could happen to a person. She didn't say it, but I knew what she really meant was what could happen to a person *like me*.

It made me sad to realize that my mother saw her youngest son in the dismembered body of a gay Asian man. But my sadness came out as irritation.

"That would never happen to me," I said, more for myself than for her.

The entire country heard about Jun Lin—his hands and feet mailed to elementary schools and political party offices—before we saw his face. And later, the face that lingered in memory was the face of his mother, the woman who crossed the Pacific Ocean to mourn her only son. Lin never came out to his mother; she only realized when another man's desire severed his body into parts.

The media reported that Lin's mother lost the will to live. She was haunted by a supposed video of his death people watched online. When Lin's mother said goodbye and put him on a plane, she didn't know what awaited him on the other side. She'd thought that Canada was a place where her son would be safe.

My mother implored me to never forget that the world is a treacherous place. She was worried that her son might too be lonely, that he might seek out that perilous intimacy.

"WHAT DID YOU SAY? *FAGGOTS!*" The hate spat out of the man's mouth with ease.

Unmoved, my partner responded by enunciating the word *nothing* with calm elegance while I sat shaking beside him.

Ten minutes earlier, we had slipped out of a dark and sweaty bar on Bloor Street West, the place where we first met and fell in love. We had been surrounded by friends, BIPOC and queer folx dancing to old-skool hip hop, bodies pressed up against each other, pressed up against the wall, dripping in the heat. Passersby would hear only bass, and looking in, they would only see shadows moving behind a fogged-up window front, and the sign *Holy Oak Café*.

We had walked a block from the café, buzzed with drink and the city, and entered a popular pizza joint. Inside were late night partygoers also looking for carbs and fat to soak up the alcohol.

The four of them—white men in sneakers—were already there, at the front of the line, deciding what to order. They took their time, so we sat down and waited. We could see that they were not satisfied with the leftover slices sitting under the glass display.

The staff—brown men in uniforms—were trying to explain that the kitchen was closed, gesticulating with their hands that nothing could be done. The four white men looked at the display counter again, and one of them pointed at the back kitchen. Everyone else in line expressed their exasperation without uttering a word, crossing their arms, turning their heads, or scanning the room to make eye contact with others who understood exactly what they felt.

Then one of the men yelled out: "Fucking Pakis!"

His friends started to leave, but he, still hungry, turned around and barked, "This is what you get for letting immigrants into this country!"

The staff stood there. Everyone else just stood there in silence.

When the white men passed us on their way out, my partner casually said, "Starve to death."

The man spun around once again. "What did you say?" He brought his face closer to ours. "WHAT DID YOU SAY? FAGGOTS!"

"Nothing."

There existed a moment when our faces could have been smashed in, but perhaps they'd already done enough damage that night. Perhaps the four of them were too stunned that someone had dared to not say nothing.

And then they left, but "Paki" and "immigrant" and "faggot" lay there on the floor like globs of cloudy phlegm.

After a stretch of silence on our walk home from the pizza joint, my partner asked, "How did he know we were gay?"

I chuckled. "Maybe because I had my hand on your thigh?"

This broke the tension, and we laughed tenderly, but I still couldn't recover from what had transpired. There's something singular about this kind of violence that estranges you from yourself. There's a shadow next to you, but you're unsure which one is self and which is shadow. You're forced to see your existence through the eyes of a hostile world.

ONCE, I WAS WALKING DOWN the street and as I passed an Asian couple going in the opposite direction, a white man on the curb yelled: "Zipperheads!" I didn't know whether he was throwing that grenade at me or the couple or all of us. He was clearly intoxicated, but he didn't fail to forget an obscure slur for Asians, one that came from the American military and that appears in one infamous Hollywood film, the same one in which Vietnamese women are depicted soliciting servicemen with the line, "Me love you long time."

The couple walked by without flinching, unaware that they might have been the intended target. I don't think anyone on the street knew that *zipperhead* originated in the Korean and Vietnam Wars, referring to the zigzag tracks left behind when tanks rolled over dead Asian bodies or the splitting open of a head when it was shot.

I continued walking and got on a streetcar, but it was going the wrong way. I forgot where I was headed and what I needed to do that afternoon. I came home later that day with milk, a bag of chips, and oranges when I needed a can of crushed tomatoes and Parmesan for the evening's pasta. I wasn't physically hurt, but *zipperhead* did what it was supposed to do, which was push me off that sidewalk, rip me from myself. The split of the zipper is a psychic one. That is its blunt and enduring power.

A readily available arsenal of words and epithets can be used to wound someone like me, even if I'm ostensibly protected from this mundane warfare because I sit in a comfortable income-tax bracket, have a PhD, and read the *New Yorker*.

And what words could I use to return fire at the man on the street or the man at the pizza joint? *Honky, white trash, cracker—* all water balloons to hand grenades.

But my partner's question leaving the pizza joint was important. How *did* he know? I didn't actually have my hand on my partner's thigh that night. We weren't holding each other or being affectionate. We were just a Vietnamese man and a Turkish man waiting for pizza. But those guys knew we were gay because we were not white, because being racialized already made us other, lesser, queer. We refused to keep our mouths shut. It didn't matter if we were gay or straight, we were faggots because we didn't leave his whiteness unchallenged. And *faggots* was only one of the number of things the man could have hurled at us. It just happened to hit home, or he knew that it would, because *faggot* is also *immigrant* is also *chink* is also *terrorist* is also *Paki* is also *foreigner*.

THE YEAR I CAME OUT, I decided to get a tattoo. I wanted to physically mark the change and to remind myself that I had a past. I wanted something that no one could destroy. I chose a hieroglyph of a boat carved onto an ancient bronze drum from Vietnam's prehistoric Đông Sơn culture. The boat was highly stylized, consisting of simple lines and dots. The image was supposed to symbolize my heritage and also commemorate my experience of being a boat refugee.

Because the early Vietnamese were a maritime people who explored the seas, travelling across the archipelago of present-day Southeast Asia, they were often involved in violent conflicts.

Looking now at the tattoo—which is wrapped around my left forearm, just below the elbow—I realize that there is no way for me to look back in history and not see the violence. To find my way back to an imagined origin is to comprehend how that origin is forged through death and destruction, not just in recent history—the war, my father's death—but also in the ancient past.

In Vietnamese, the word *nước* means both "water" and "country, homeland, or nation." The idea of a community of people growing rice, sharing language, and launching boats is rooted in water. But in the aftermath of war, water was the means by which many of these people were separated from their community, when they desperately took to boats in search of new beginnings.

WHEN MY MOTHER FIRST SAW my forearm, she told me to stop getting tattoos.

She and I were sitting inside a small restaurant in Calgary's Little Saigon, a complex of strip malls meant to re-create a past world. She knew the owner, so they made chit-chat while I stared out the window, where the South Vietnamese heritage flag was flapping in tandem with a Canadian flag at a four-way intersection. This was the closest to Vietnam we had been in a long time.

I was hungry, so I ordered vermicelli and rice crepes. My mother only wanted a small bowl of chicken phở. When the owner left, my mother turned back to me and commented on his daughter nearby. "That girl used to be really fat."

I made a face of annoyance. We sat in silence and waited for our food, each stuck in our own small existence.

When her food arrived, she chewed slowly and carefully. Everything she does is done with so much care, each movement weary from the one that came before, wary of the one to come after. I tried to eat as fast as I could, swallowing every bite whole.

As we were finishing up, two men entered the restaurant and stood discussing their upcoming fishing trip. My mother looked up. "How enjoyable it is to go fishing in old age." Her voice trailed across the room.

This time, I couldn't resist. "Mom, can you please not talk about people in front of them?"

She responded by pivoting her body to the window and the world outside, as if looking for a distant memory neither of us remembered existed. There was no expression of resentment or hurt. There was just my mother, whom I desired to both hold and run away from.

I GREW UP THINKING THAT my father's absence was the foundation of my being. I defined myself as a fatherless person; my longing, my melancholy, my isolation from the world were all a result of living with his death. I spent years searching for him in stories that others told and in my own faulty memory.

All the while, my mother clothed and fed me; she yelled at me and hit me with a feather duster when I misbehaved; she picked mushrooms, cleaned toilets, and made sandwiches to earn money.

I remember watching her get ready for work one morning when I was a teenager and realizing that she had been wearing the same sweater for more than ten years. There were holes in it, ones she could not, or did not have the time to, patch up.

She was dealt a life not many people could survive, and in the process of living it she became the person I know of as my mother.

But I don't know her.

My father I can invent. There is no reality—no unfolding life—to contradict the way I imagine him: the happy-go-lucky man who could drink anyone under the table, the devoted husband and father, the parent who would indulge me or talk me out of trouble. My father is a static fiction I've long preserved.

My mother I've had to live with and continue to discover over time. She has the potential to surprise me still, to disrupt any narrative I form about myself and our lives. And I must reconcile her immense courage with the woman who sits across the table from me, casually observing others. This mother could easily drift away without me noticing.

I never had to look for my mother because she was always there.

ON ONE OF MY VISITS to Calgary after I came out, we sat in the living room together. My mother was channel surfing while I worked on my laptop. I was at the halfway point of a two-week stay and was ready to return to my life in Toronto. I couldn't wait to get away. But I also knew that the moment I stepped foot inside the airport, something inside me would crack, and I'd want to be right by her side again.

When I looked up from my screen, I saw her staring at the TV, cozy underneath a cheap synthetic blanket, watching as the bachelor gave someone a rose.

When I began writing about my mother, I didn't know how much I didn't know. Instead of asking her to tell me her story, I thought I'd watch her from a short distance and record moments of our life together. I reasoned that this was safer. I was afraid I'd learn things I wasn't ready to know or if we began to talk, I too would have to confess parts of myself.

A while ago, missing my mother but not wanting to reach out, I sketched this image of her:

> She sits on the carpeted floor leafing through a huge pile of flyers. Her hunched back looks like half of an unfinished bridge. Her eyes squint as she brings an opened flyer up to her face to have a closer look. She says, to no one, "They are selling rice cookers for $9.99 at Canadian Tire! Is it true?" She begins clipping coupons that she will never use.

Like my mother, I've become an observer of others, a commentator who sits on the sidelines. I clip small, everyday moments of her so I can piece them together and make her more than what she is, but never everything she means to me.

8

HOUSTON

IF I HAD KNOWN, I would have brought flowers. Or a pack of Marlboro Red and a case of Heineken. I would have sat cross-legged in front of the large wall lined with wooden tablets naming the deceased, lit a cigarette, and popped a chilled bottle in offering to him. I would have said, "Cheers, Father." A lifelong pilgrimage come to a fitting conclusion.

"Một, hai, ba, dzô."

I didn't know, when my aunt suggested that we visit the Buddhist temple on our first morning in Houston, that she was taking me and my siblings to meet our father. More accurately, that she was bringing us to his resting place, the earthly spot where his spirit resides.

The temple was a large complex of buildings, set off from the main road. Shaded by oaks and pines, it was designed to evoke sanctuary, a retreat from the troubles and suffering of everyday life. Through the entrance gate, topped with a red dharma wheel and colourful prayer flags, was the double-roofed grand hall. This was where ceremonies were performed, where people came to pay their respects, beseech the spirits, and see off the dead.

Pointing to a side building, my aunt casually said, "Your father is in there." As if I could walk in and see him standing there with his arms wide open.

"What?" I blurted as our car doors slammed shut and the Texas summer pressed down against the back of my throat, constricting the passage of air. It felt like being baked alive.

I was in Houston for a reunion with my father's side of the family. I hadn't seen any of them in decades, because we were spread all over the place, and bringing a family scattered by war together is a difficult thing to do. The idea for a gathering started when my father's sister said to my mother over the phone that she had stories she wanted to tell me, and I told my mother that I wanted to hear them. They decided on August 2022, a month before I would turn forty.

A plan was made for me to come visit, and then that plan ballooned to a full-fledged reunion including various aunts and uncles, siblings and cousins. There were, of course, some family members who could not attend, but it would be the first time this many of us came together in one place.

It was also the first time I would meet my father's siblings as an adult, as someone who recognized the significance of who they were.

I anticipated this meeting knowing they were keepers of untold histories and mundane knowledge of someone whom I didn't know. They understood the man behind the myth I had conjured. They would provide me with details to plaster the gaps in the crumbling family home inside my mind.

In her living room the night before the temple visit, just hours after our arrival, my aunt spoke about a real, physical house, the one my grandparents had to vacate when they were displaced farther southward for the third or fourth time during the war, the last property they ever owned. There was a mango tree that drooped with ripening fruit in the back of that house, which sat near the water in Quy Nhơn in central Vietnam. The breeze, when it came, blew in through the back door and out the front windows. With the loss of that house, the family became fragmented—one person lived here, and another lived there. They were never all together again.

In Saigon, because my grandparents were not on the government registry, because they were refugees, they could not secure a place to live. After many nervous inquiries as they wandered from neighbourhood to neighbourhood, a generous family friend allowed them to stay in the small extension—a shack really—of their property. In this shack, as the birds chittered on top of the corrugated-tin roof dappled with the leaves' moving shadows, my grandfather, after roaming the streets selling lottery tickets one morning, died during his afternoon nap.

My uncle, my father's youngest brother, then jumped into the conversation. He regaled us with his tale of arriving in the United States alone, working any and all odd jobs, sharing a room with five other men like him, sending every dollar back so his mother could buy a house. He'd lie awake at night inside his aching body, dreaming of writing poetry and putting lines to music. His most gorgeous poem will be the two-storey concrete building he labours into possession for his mother, a place for her to die inside. A song that will be sung forever.

Another uncle sat there and remained silent. It was hard to imagine this man—the handsomest in the family, the scholar with the movie star looks, imprisoned in the re-education camps for over a decade, and then migrating to the United States to work at making women's feet look pretty with red nail polish—now living a life of solitude in a retirement village.

I looked from one to the other, wondering what ancient heartbreak stitched these siblings together, the ones present and the ones already gone, like a tattered chain of paper dolls holding hands.

"They, those Việt Cộng," my aunt picked up the conversation, "they made your father give up your family's house. In his desperation to leave, he tried every possible way. He bribed an official with the house," she said. "He exchanged it for a future with you." She pointed at me, not in an accusing way, but in a way that said, Here you are, a manifestation of your father's enduring love.

"Was he homeless in the final months of his life in Vietnam?" I asked.

My aunt sighed, "Without his family, he had no need for a house, he had no home to go back to."

INSIDE THE FUNERARY BUILDING, I searched for my father among hundreds of mass-produced tablets. They all had the same look, painted a shiny mahogany brown: a carved lotus-flower base, a tabula body with a portrait of the deceased and the dates of their birth and departure, and a flying-eaves roof to ward off evil. A shelter for the soul, each tablet represents a body that once lived in this world.

When I found him, I saw that he was next to his father, where he belonged.

Was there a space next to him for me?

I put my palms together and bowed three times, walked a full circle around the large statue of a seated Buddha, then exited.

Crossing over the threshold, I said silently to myself: Goodbye.

Outside, I heard the oscillating buzz of cicadas emerging from the soil to reproduce and then die.

It seemed strange to me, at that moment, that my father's spirit was not with my mother in Calgary. But then again, I lived far away from family too. I knew that distance wasn't the measure of love. Distance was sometimes what made love possible.

I was glad my father had a home in Houston, even if he was separated from our family. I wondered, in the blinding afternoon sun, if my father's spirit ever travelled to Canada. Do the deceased have compasses to navigate their way back to us?

THAT EVENING, AFTER DINNER, EVERYONE crammed knee to knee around the dining table. More chairs were squeezed in between chairs, and butts shifted over to make space. Some of us sat in the cracks between two seats or on the edge of someone else's chair, not falling only because of their loving grip. We wanted to feel this closeness that we'd missed out on for so many years. We knew this was the best—indeed, the only—way for people like us to begin sharing with each other.

Food was replenished and more food added to the already overflowing table: lychees, boiled peanuts, sweet sticky rice, mangoes, beef jerky, longans, candied coconut, dried squid, banana cookies, and kumquats. Limbs reached to grab at the bounty or to pass the best pieces over to others, to scoop, to hold, break open; fingers feeding mouths; legs and feet criss-crossing. The chaotic choreography of being together.

Existing as a part of this family felt like old times, even though we'd never done this before. We became closer to each other and also closer to our past selves—those longing refugees sticking together to protect each other. It was as if everything in the intervening years, and everything we'd managed to achieve—the degrees, the professional careers, the big houses—and our failures—the foreclosed businesses, the divorces, the missed opportunities—all ceased to matter. This, at the core, was who we really were.

The words and teasing, the affectionate touching, the unity allowed us to lose ourselves in each other. It made me nervous to melt into this thing called family.

I was the first to leave, quietly moving to the sofa in the living room, where I could lean back and watch them.

And they watched me too.

"Doesn't he look so much like brother Cấn," my uncle asked. "Exactly like him," my aunt replied. Together, they scrutinized my appearance, pointing out similarities and differences between me, an aging man about to turn forty, and my father, a man who had died in his forties. They made me stand up. "The length of his legs, thin and hairy," they judged, "is identical," patting me on the bum as if I were a child. They pointed out, "The ears are uncanny." "The eyes," they said, "have the same shape, the same sad look, but your father's were bigger." Touching my nose, they said, "His was more elegant." But, they concluded, walking along the street on a foggy night, anyone could mistake me for my reincarnated father.

"Just like your father," they said.

Everyone nodded in agreement.

But they were not the only ones who scrutinized. In the days that followed, I observed and tried to notice everything. I made note of them in my mind, cataloguing information about each of them. I made copies of this living archive:

The deep timbre of their sophisticated northern accent, the way their hands chopped the air when they spoke, the tilt of their heads, the cheekbones protruding when they smiled, the affectionate teasing, the booming laughter, the witty wordplay, the lewd jokes of one uncle, the lonely introspection of another, the stubborn love of one aunt, sinewy arms, arched backs, thighs shaking while seated, full lips stretching wide, dark sunspots, lines in the corner of the eyes, the tragedies that have been lived, the desire for vengeance they all shared against the Communists who destroyed everything they knew.

I told myself I was creating an imperfect facsimile of my father—what he might have been if he could have reached old age, if time had had the chance to do its work on his mind and body. I built him out of the parts I saw in my aunt and uncles. A Frankenstein father resurrected during a family reunion.

We all got to meet my father one more time.

We knew that we were not him.

He is forever gone.

· · ·

THE NEXT MORNING, WE DROVE to Baytown to escape the heat wave, and to let the younger family members catch fish fed by the muddy waters of the Trinity River.

Twenty-five refugees and their descendants packed into five vehicles and headed to a two-bedroom beach house. It seemed like a challenge to fit everyone into the house, yet we were never crowded; we always managed to find enough space, putting a blow-up bed here, rearranging a couch there, squeezing one more body into a bunk bed. The cool, moist breeze from the gulf relaxed our bodies and lulled our minds into rest. Some of us took naps that afternoon, splayed out in the living room.

While the women laid newspaper on the kitchen floor and split open a giant jackfruit, its golden flesh like jewels inside a geode, I sat at the table drinking beer with the men. I took this opportunity to broach the topic of war.

I walked around it slowly at first, afraid of stepping on an unexploded land mine. Or worse, I worried that my uncles would put up their defences and keep me locked outside what they knew.

I began by asking light questions about military rankings, battalions, and training. And then, when they let their guards down, I asked them to tell me what fighting a war was like, if they had ever come close to being killed, if they'd ever killed a man.

Someone brought a bowl stacked with plump, glowing jackfruits to the table. The fruits felt cool and sticky in between our bony, wrinkled fingers. We sat, savouring the ripeness of the sun on our silent tongues.

Minutes passed.

When words came back to them, my uncles told me that what I might know was very small.

You may be a professor, and you may have read many books, they intimated, but don't ever think that these books give you the full story, *our story*. The one we lived. What you've read in books about people like us, men who defended the fallen nation of South Vietnam, cannot be trusted. They, the Americans, they, the Communists, wrote stories about us, but because we have no country, no land and water, we have no one to tell our history, no place to pass it on.

"What you know, and how you've come to know it, is wrong," they said.

I nodded.

I told them I was writing stories about Vietnam, and about our lives. They didn't recoil, or object, or say, "Ha! What is there to write about your measly years on this planet? What good is your story?"

We sat in silence.

It was not exactly an endorsement from my uncles, but I felt, at that moment, some licence had opened up for me to write about big and complicated things.

"You need to understand," they said, "that what your story needs is *history*."

"You cannot write what we went through if you don't know what our country, our people, had to endure."

"Tell your story, but make sure to get our history right," they cautioned.

ONE DAY, SHORTLY AFTER THE trip to Houston, I looked over an old draft of something I'd written and saw a comment from an early reader. She'd advised that my story needed more historical details for it to come alive. What my story required, she told me, was the larger significance that the war could provide. Readers needed a reason to care about what happened to my father and to me. Readers would be more invested if I connected my story directly to the lasting impact of the war.

I started to think about this advice, which was not so different from my uncles' caution to get history right.

But what did it mean to get history *right*? Under the enormous weight of all that's been written about the Vietnam War—it is, according to one respected historian, the most documented war in US historiography—what history-writing was possible within my little story?

I began by going to the library to search for books I hadn't read and to reread the ones I had. I took meticulous notes on pads of yellow paper and drew diagrams showing important events. The facts of war slowly came together in my head, but sitting down to write, I still experienced a sinking inadequacy. Something crucial was missing. A felt understanding, beyond the facts, eluded me.

I had to admit that I didn't know history.

And I could never know it the way my uncles wanted me to. I could never give readers the history they needed.

That's when I decided I would simply make it up. Instead of squeezing my small story into the grand annals of history, I would make history fit into *my* story. I would turn my desires into an incomplete record of what happened to Vietnam during the twentieth century. I would provide context through fiction and historical details through characters. Recount events via plot and render decisions in feeling. Embellish and animate everything.

I would resurrect my father and conjure my mother as star-crossed characters in an age-old epic, dramatize history through their developing romance, because stories of war are, at their core, love stories gone wrong.

Part II

WHAT HAPPENED

9

A MADE-UP HISTORY

THE BORROWED SUIT HANGS LIKE a deflated man pinned against the door frame.

An ominous sign—but the man who will wear it is unaware. Known as Nguyễn the Patriot, and later as Hồ Chí Minh, he is studiously writing a letter at his desk. In the flickering light of the oil lamp, he's trying to express something about freedom and self-determination, equality and inalienable rights. Life, Liberty, and the pursuit of Happiness: he will utter these very words decades later as he declares his country independent of French colonial rule in front of a rapturous crowd in Hanoi's Ba Đình Square. Approaching the microphone, he will shade his eyes from the sun with cupped hands while white light glistens off the eager faces of his people—unlike on this lonely, damp night in Paris.

On that future day of independence in 1945, Việt Nam, his beloved, will be born again. Not Her first birth, because She's always had to reinvent herself, stave off men who wanted to possess Her, who occupied Her lands and violated Her body for tin, coal, and rubber. Men who starved and tortured Her children.

Hồ Chí Minh's love for Việt Nam comes from seeing Her hands in manacles, knowing that the Chinese ruled Her for three centuries, and the French for one, and then the Japanese, as the world scrambled to redraw its borders. When humanity is reborn after years of bullets, blitzes, and alliances; years of Holocaust; and the final catastrophe of the A-bomb, the man thinks his country will be free.

But imperialists never give up so easily what they see as their rightful property, and this lecherous greed attracts the attention of other men—allies who fought in a world war together, defenders of capitalist democracies and of each other's interest. This small, shapely country will become the site of a hot war within a cold one. Her next suitor will be the Americans, who see Her as a domino in a vital game, a block that must not fall and set off a chain reaction, spreading red Communism.

To curtail this spread, these men will sever Her into two: North and South. She will remain that way for over two decades—broken, at odds with Herself.

That lands—and nations, peoples, and psyches—can be halved and quartered is why men think of them as women, as someone to love and fight for, conquer, and then leave. It's a tired trope, but it reveals much about man's possessive imagination and his relationship to war and peace.

Getting up to stretch his tired limbs, Hồ Chí Minh looks out the window. A shaft of streetlight catches two figures embracing in the encroaching fog. He can make out one set of masculine hands, but the other figure is hidden by the night.

He reaches for his heating brick to warm his stiff, cold fingers. He thinks about the tingle pineapple leaves in the mouth—pineapple shares the same word as *fragrant* in his native tongue.

Việt Nam will remain the only woman in his life. He's married to his ideal, his supporters will say.

When Việt Nam becomes whole again in 1975, at the war's end, it will be by force and bloodshed. The revolution he dreams of will happen after his death, in slow and painful ways, in exchange for three million lives.

Sitting down again at his desk, back stooped from a learned determination, he continues working on his letter. That it, and many others, will reach no one is not a matter of importance. Tomorrow, when Hồ Chí Minh puts on the borrowed suit, the inch-too-long cuff will escape his notice. This unassuming man will become the heroic Uncle Hồ of the nation that won't be conquered. What will be remembered is that he charged on toward the lighted horizon of freedom.

• • •

IN 1945, MY FATHER IS only two years old and my grandfather cradles him in his arms, listening to Uncle Hồ declare independence. My grandfather hears every word with trepidation, knowing that bags must be packed soon, because Communism—the proposed nationalist solution to decolonization—does not arouse hope in everyone. It doesn't completely sweep the country up in its grand embrace.

In about a decade, when the nation is divided at the seventeenth parallel, millions of people will journey southward to settle elsewhere. This is the first wave of refugees the war will create, a massive caravan of internal migrants, many of whom will become displaced again when the war ends.

Like all men of his generation, my father will join the war, but he and Uncle will not fight on the same side. Instead, they will end up bitter enemies.

IN THE FINAL YEAR OF the turbulent 1960s, my father is a lieutenant in the military. He's twenty-seven, tall, handsome in his fatigues, and his black boots give him a matured masculinity. The ladies notice him.

But he already has his eyes on someone. A few months ago, on a return visit to Quy Nhơn, where his family resettled from the North in 1954 after the battle at Điện Biên Phủ, a young woman caught his eye.

He ran into a friend, and that friend introduced him to other friends, and as they drank beer at a busy streetside watering hole, she appeared.

She walked arm in arm with a girlfriend on the sidewalk. Something amusing was said, and they turned toward each other in intimate laughter. A slight breeze passed through the black hair that hung over her shoulders. She wore a green cardigan over her áo dài, which billowed behind her.

This was how my mother entered his world. Everything else surrounding her blurred out and sped up; only she remained sharp, in slow motion, for his eyes to behold.

When time resumed, he was hit with the terrible realization that she would exit the frame, and his life, forever. But as it happened, her elder brother was sitting next to my father. He waved at his sister, who approached and greeted everyone politely.

She was a vertical, light drizzle in the hottest of dry months.

My father couldn't be sure, but in his mind, she looked him in the eyes and smiled. The roundness of her face, the porcelain tint of her skin, the slender shape of her figure beneath the tight dress sent him spinning.

Not long after that, he enlisted his mother to engage a matchmaker, and they arrived at my mother's house to ask for her hand in marriage. This was the beginning of their romance.

On March 23, 1969, my mother's twenty-first birthday, my father gets into his jeep and drives along the coast. He's on his way to meet his fiancée. It's only their third date, and he takes her first to the garden, where the flowers are just beginning to bloom. She says to him in a gentle voice, "How lovely it is to be in a place where the scent of frangipani fills the air." He nods in agreement, enraptured by this woman who will soon be his to hold.

From the garden, they walk toward the beach, where my father tells her to take off her slippers and dig her toes into the warm sand. He carries her slippers for her, and they dangle off his long fingers, a hook against the clear horizon. As they meander parallel to the water, these two young lovers hear little waves crashing against the shore and tiny voices of nearby children erupting in delight. With sudden bravery, my father takes my mother's hand in his, and it seems that they have all the time in the world.

AT THE MOMENT THEIR HANDS touch, somewhere in North Vietnam, the land is being bombed. Boeing B-52s fill the skies like winged monsters, dropping missiles carrying massive amounts of explosives. As ordnances hit the ground, blinding flashes of orange streak the landscape before plumes of smoke rise to hang over everything. This scene occurs over and over again, stretching across acres of scarred land. For a time, as one American military leader proclaims, the country is bombed back to the Stone Age. Bombed out of time.

An escaping villager, trying to shield her child from the fire in the sky, blurts out, moments before total annihilation, "There is no longer time. There is no time."

These bombings will continue for another six years, until 1975. They will get more ferocious and extend along what Americans call the Ho Chi Minh Trail, a network of roads cutting through jungles, used by the Communists to transport materials southward in support of the Việt Cộng. These bombings will clandestinely spill over into Cambodia and Laos, pulling them into the war.

When the skies clear, over 6.8 million tons of explosives will have been dropped within a matter of years, more than in the entirety of the Second World War. It will go down as the largest aerial bombardment in history, and the small Southeast Asian region as the most heavily bombed place on earth.

It won't end there. These bombs will live on. Many of them will not explode when they first hit the ground. They will lie dormant, like the trauma that will take hold in the bodies of those who survive. They will wait for some innocent boy scavenging scrap metal to trade for a few American dollars. Everything that touches one of these bombs will burst. The earth will shake again, and the sky will rumble. Human mouths will scream a terrifying scream of dread, of terror, of madness. The innocent boy and many like him will vanish from this world.

The war is not over. The war continues to kill. We have yet to know how many lives it will claim, whether by bomb or gunfire or drowning or grief.

• • •

ONE OF THESE LIVES WILL be my father's, but as my mother kisses him on the cheek before heading to her classroom, neither of them know the fate that awaits them.

We keep on living precisely because we don't know what will happen, my mother will tell her children one day. But today is just another day of not knowing—the sun in a cloudless sky, the air heavy with moisture.

My mother leaves her two daughters with the nanny, because a woman can have a profession and independence too, in this politically unstable Việt Nam.

My father, mother, and sisters live now in Saigon—a city that was once a wild marsh, settled by an ancient kingdom, invaded by the Vietnamese, and controlled by the French. Its name stands for "wood" and "cotton," but it will be renamed after the war's end for the father of the nation, Hồ Chí Minh.

In the early 1970s, Saigon is the bustling centre of the war economy, where important men congregate, news travels by wire, and money is spent. At night, the streets fill with women in skirts and bell bottoms, families enjoying ice cream on a stroll, street hawkers pushing wares, and American GIs on furlough. Rock 'n' roll can be heard blasting from the bars, while English and Vietnamese tongues mix against the sounds of exploding exhaust pipes.

My mother does not like the humid heat of Saigon, but she enjoys her new teaching position at the high school on Trương Minh Giảng Street. She is known for her fairness, and the students understand not to deceive someone so conscientious, who asks them to, above all, be honest.

Today she asks her students to compose a piece on the future of Việt Nam. She already knows what they will write and how they will write it. Every essay will begin with the threat Communism poses and end with the hope for freedom. Freedom. That word again. Everyone wants it, but no one can agree on what it means in Việt Nam. In her students' essays, everything about themselves will be left out.

What she really wants to ask is, What do you dream of? What future do you see for yourself in all this mess? Who will you become?

She looks up from her desk to see her students sitting in rows, their shoulders bent in concentration, and she realizes that what she wants is to ask those questions of herself.

While her students write, a breeze ruffles the pages of those closest to the opened window. She gets up to close it and sees a fighter jet leaving behind a trail as it zips across the empty sky. She has a sudden craving for ripe, golden pineapple and calculates, again, how many weeks she is late, worried about the possible life growing inside her.

As she thinks this, over ten thousand kilometres away in Paris, the day is just drawing to a close. It's a momentous day— what many will refer back to as the beginning of the end. It took years of negotiation to reach this moment.

The sky is grey and gloomy. Reporters and protesters huddle under umbrellas, while men in suits sit at a large round table inside the Hotel Majestic. They sign sheafs of paper passed along to them, promising peace and cessation. Two men, one American and one Việt Cộng, will receive the Nobel Peace Prize for facilitating this process. One will accept; the other will decline. The prize committee will have had to forget how both men made peace via the promulgation of violence.

When the last scratch of pen touches paper, they all stand up in solemn exhaustion. Any celebration later on that night—the smiles, the clinking of glasses, the music—will be done for the sake of the media.

A few months later, the last American troops withdraw from Việt Nam. They will write this withdrawal as honourable, as a fitting conclusion to their heroic sojourn into the jungles of world history.

THE REAL END, THE PRESIDENTIAL Palace knows, doesn't arrive until two years later, on April 30, 1975, when a Russian-made T-54 tank crashes into and breaks open its iron gates. The Palace has seen so much and remembers what has passed through it. A place has memory too. It absorbs everything that happens and carries history forward in time.

The Palace remembers that it once had another frame and that in 1962, two dissident South Vietnamese pilots attempted an assassination of the president by bombing its left wing. The injuries the Palace suffered led to its reconstruction from a neo-baroque building, when it was used by the colonial governor of French Cochinchina, to its current brutalist style, used by the leaders of the Republic of South Vietnam.

The Palace has seen it all: women in ball gowns and men in top hats, the best soufflés served to visiting dignitaries, secret trysts between the native help and their desirous employers, decision-makers in closed-door meetings, telephone calls exchanging classified information, military drills, shots fired, madams and children rushing into underground bomb shelters.

On its head is a helipad, ready for the president and his family to escape by air.

On April 30, North Vietnamese soldiers run through its halls waving the revolutionary flag, declaring an end to war. This is when it becomes the Independence Palace.

On this historic day, the Palace takes a curious peek across its lawn, down the large boulevard, and out into the city. What it sees is chaos. The scene looks nothing like liberation or fall, freedom or defeat, just ordinary people scrambling to make it to another day: A man rushing home on his bicycle. A young girl pulling her sisters along the street to find their parents. A woman carrying a purse full of gold she knows will be her only way to survive. A man on his knees, his head in his hands, crying. Five children sharing a tiny baguette. Discarded semi-automatics and boots. More tanks crawling down the street. The air buzzing with uncertainty. Dipterocarp trees swaying in mimicry of surrender.

If it were able to extend its vision a bit farther, the Palace would see a Citröen being set on fire, along with the documents and photographs inside. It would see black smoke rising into the sky. A man with a pistol positioned against the side of his head. Soldiers shoving onlookers to the side. People running away—from what and to where, they do not know.

It would see suitcases and packed bags being thrown over a sea of bobbing heads. Limbs reaching forward, bent in awkward positions. Bodies pressed upon bodies, pressed upon bodies, becoming one giant mass bursting through the cell walls of the American embassy, jostling for a precious seat on departing helicopters.

At the mouth of an alley nearby, my father and pregnant mother watch this scene. They know it's too late to even try, so they just stand there as the world they know slowly crumbles apart. They both realize that many things need to be done immediately: documents discarded, jewellery hidden, children consoled, letters written, new identities to assume. Change always takes you by the throat.

Nothing they see shocks them, but they can't be certain this is their Saigon. They knew it was coming—the news and rumours, the panicked goodbyes, the president who fled his Palace a few days earlier. But it all seems far away, like a foreign film about themselves that they are watching but can't understand.

What wakes them is my mother's purse being snatched from her arm. When they realize what has happened, my parents blink their eyes to see a young boy hobbling away on one leg, dragging a much-too-big crutch on the uneven concrete road. The laboured way his body moves forces them to imagine the coming years of this new Vietnam.

Neither of them chases after the boy.

. . .

THE BOY IS WHAT MANY call "the dust of life," those with nothing and nothing to lose. Long ago, when the boy had a family, he lost his left leg when he woke in the middle of the night to relieve himself. As he emerged from the dark outhouse, a bullet sliced through the air and pierced his thigh. The boy cried out in terror and collapsed. Finding him on the dirt floor, his mother wrapped his leg and ran all night to the nearest town, where the doctor said there was no other choice. The boy was lucky he hadn't bled to death.

The boy's family lived in a small village that was liberated by South Vietnamese troops during the day and recaptured by the Việt Cộng during the night, over and over again. In the midst of this constant shuttling between freedom and occupation, occupation and freedom, the villagers tilled the earth and bred pigs. They did not know who was their enemy and who was their protector, just the caprice of the gods who provided rain or drought.

One day, their village was burned to the ground, either to cut off the supply of food for the Việt Cộng or to prevent the South Vietnamese army from recruiting new soldiers. So the boy and his family ended up in Saigon, and a cruel twist of fate sent his parents flying through the air when a car smashed into their rusty bicycle carrying two tiny adults and a bamboo coop full of chickens. Feathers fell like confetti.

On the day the boy steals my mother's purse, he does not even know that the war has ended. He does not care what will happen to Vietnam.

Two months from that day, nothing has changed for him. He's still barely alive, and he still scours the sidewalks for discarded food, which has become almost non-existent. He does have a new family, headed by a twenty-seven-year-old, fresh-faced gangster. This family begs on the street, and when begging doesn't work, they pull out their knives in back alleys. Because paper money is no longer valuable, they look for the watch or the ring, the precious piece of metal that will sell on the black market, which is the only market left.

Roaming the streets, these brothers see boarded-up storefronts, houses confiscated by the government, and suspicion on people's faces. In neighbourhoods, children are asked to spy on their parents, neighbours report on each other, and dissidents are denounced in public. It isn't enough that the economy has collapsed, that parts of the city have no electricity or running water, that rows of buildings lie in shambles. People must also betray others to survive.

The gang turns into a small alley, where they see a Buddhist temple and pass my father, no longer young, haggard from history, exiting his house.

Two weeks earlier, my father received a letter asking him to come to a "meeting." These ten-day meetings, organized by the new government, are meant to rehabilitate those involved with the fallen regime. The men who voluntarily register will complete the meeting and be assimilated back into the new society. Reasoning that it's better to go now than wait to be forced later, my father has packed his bags and promised his children he will return soon. They hug and kiss, not knowing that ten days will turn into seven years. No one can imagine that my father will be jammed into a truck with other men and sent to remote parts of the country to build the camps imprisoning them, dig ditches and wells, clear jungle, and sweep the land for unexploded mines.

As my father squeezes into the back of the military truck that will take him away, a dog appears. This mutt of unknown origins will outlive many of the men inside the truck. As the truck begins to move, the dog watches and barks into the waxing dusk.

The dog had an owner, a merchant of Chinese background, and lived in utter comfort. She was loved by the family, especially the eldest daughter, who would, without fail, feed her under the table. Abalone, pork belly, and cubes of stir-fried beef were her favourite.

When the family got on one of the final boats leaving Saigon, they left many precious things behind, including the young dog.

For weeks, she stayed inside the empty house, waiting for her owners to return. When the police, who were until recently young boys in black pajamas and rubber sandals squatting in the jungle, arrived to claim the house as theirs, they marvelled at the modern contraption called a "toilet," and kicked the dog in the behind, out the door.

The dog spent the next two months roaming the streets. One evening, a kind man gave her a chicken bone and patted her on the head. He brought her home and gave her a warm corner to sleep in. Early the next morning, the dog woke to a sharp sound, and something just didn't feel right. Before the man was able to get the leash around her head, she bit his hand and crashed through the door.

When she sees the truck taking away my father, she has just escaped becoming the next meal. She will meet her end years from then, inside a fancy veterinary clinic, after the doctor has tried every expensive procedure to treat her ailing liver.

TWO YEARS AFTER WATCHING THE dust settle on the road as the truck drove off, the dog, who now has seen everything and survived, encounters a French journalist, one of the few the Vietnamese government has allowed into the new country to write about its successful reconstruction. They meet on the steps of the Opera House, when she approaches him and licks the coconut juice dripping from his hand. The journalist instantly falls in love and takes the dog with him back to Paris, and then a year later to Montreal, where he resettles.

One snowy evening, the dog, who has a new name—Chabichou, because of her smooth coat—is lying next to the journalist on the sofa. On the blaring television, men in suits are having a furious debate. When she hears the word

Vietnam, her ears perk up and a wave of nostalgia for tropical nights and spiced meats overcomes her. She cannot understand the conversation about the syndrome; about Vietnam afflicting America; about military failure and national decline; about the need to fight more wars and to win, most importantly to win; about the noble cause; about the malaise that must be overcome. America needs to heal from Vietnam, the men claim. The war has caused a major rift in its society, a dent in its self-confidence, a blemish in its record of foundational violence.

When one of the men raises his voice and slams his hand on the table, producing a sharp thump, the dog gets on her hind legs and raises her back. The journalist sees that she is tense. She starts to bark, first slowly, then with more rage. The journalist holds her and tries to calm her down, but she is inconsolable. Everything she's experienced comes back. To get away, she bites the journalist's arm and runs toward the door, slamming her body over and over against its immovable threshold.

When she dies, the journalist is distraught. He's never been more alone in his life, and he begins to take stock of what it has all meant, what covering war did for others and what it did to him. On one particularly dark night he takes a Colt .45-calibre pistol from his enormous collection of firearms and places it under his chin. He would never actually do it, but in this moment, he wants to know what it would feel like. He wants to sense how things could end.

• • •

THE PISTOL WAS MADE IN Connecticut in the 1970s. From there it travelled to Vietnam and was assigned to a nineteen-year-old grunt from Kansas tasked with seeking out enemies hidden in subterranean tunnels. On its most glorious day, the pistol killed eight Việt Cộng disguising themselves as villagers. When its eye met those of its victims, the pistol felt nothing but thirst. *More, more, more* is the translation for *bang, bang, bang.*

The pistol didn't stay with the grunt for long. One oppressively hot night in the mosquito-occupied jungle, he became possessed by wanton spirits. The grunt walked into a clearing, stuck the pistol into his mouth, and prayed for mercy. What the pistol saw was emptiness.

The pistol got reassigned to someone else and then someone else, and it did more killing. Nothing interesting to recount. Just *more, more, more.*

It ended up in the hands of a South Vietnamese commander. On April 30, 1975, as the Việt Cộng entered Saigon to claim it as their own, the commander grabbed an enemy prisoner, dragged him into the street, and shot him in the head. The commander asked everyone present to witness his lack of cowardice, and then he shot himself in the head too, because the pistol demanded *more.*

When the journalist bought the pistol at a shop selling medals and lighters, helmets and guns, the pistol thought it had already retired. For many years with the journalist, it enjoyed the life of peace and calm, much like the powerful men who blazingly waged war only to retreat into gardening, painting, or babysitting in neatly ordered suburban homes.

Fate would have it that when the journalist passed away, the pistol was sold into a drug ring, crossed the border, boarded a ship, and made its way back to Southeast Asia with a group of resettled refugees in the United States, who wanted to continue fighting, to "restore" the lost Vietnamese homeland.

The pistol's last years are spent with a Cambodian smuggler, who guides refugees by boat to Thailand. While these refugees carry with them gold, dollars, and dreams, the most precious item on board is always the pistol. The pistol can command order, can scare away opportunists, can buy everyone some time to swim or run.

On this its final night, the pistol extends its rigid body into the air, waving vigorously to those running from the bushes toward the docking boat. It does not know that in mere hours it will end up on the sea floor after being carried away by the current, knocking up against drifting frozen bodies.

The pistol's fate will join that of hundreds of thousands of refugees who fled postwar Vietnam. On this breezy April night in 1989, the pistol will sit in the same boat as my father, who has made it this far, crossing over from Vietnam. The farthest he will get in this life.

* * *

Two days before this moment, my father wakes up as if it's just another morning. He dresses in the dark and feels his way from one room to another. At the door, he picks up the small bag he packed the night before, filled with what, he can no longer recall.

Quietly, while his sister and her children sleep, he slips on a pair of plastic slippers—bright orange—that does not belong to him, and walks out. As he makes his way to the meeting point, where a truck is already waiting, the swollen violet of early dawn colours him blue.

He gets into the truck with other men also carrying small bags. They stay silent for the duration of the ride to the Cambodian border, contemplating their first opportunity to back out.

When they arrive in Phnom Penh, my father wanders the night alone, eating a steaming bowl of noodles and buying a small trinket at the market. He sits on a little stool and smokes an entire pack of cigarettes. He does not sleep.

The next day, he and the others are transported to a small town by the edge of Kampong Som bay, where they are hidden beneath the floorboards of a house.

Under the cover of darkness, they are dropped off by the water and told to wait in the bushes. A woman with two small children asks my father to hold her infant son. She wants him, when the time comes, to get the infant safely across the hungry swamp.

My father holds the boy in silence. It is his last chance to turn back.

When the smuggler waves his pistol in the air, my father runs toward the water carrying the child. The mud swallows his feet, and the tree roots try to hold him back.

But he pushes his strained body forward to reach the boat, where he hands the infant to outstretched hands. When he gets himself onto the boat, something inside him lifts. He is weightless as the boat begins to move.

A night of sailing, and I will be free, he thinks to himself. When the sun rises, I will see the coast of Thailand. He is determined. In the camp, we will be reunited. He grins as the sea breaks against a side of the boat, spraying everyone on board in the face.

The boat moves forward in absolute darkness, guided by experience and fuelled by hope. Nobody can tell where the sky ends and the water begins. Nobody can tell if it has been an hour or an interminable lifetime. The smell of gasoline fills their nostrils and makes them light-headed.

When they see a red light blinking in the distance is also when the boat starts to rock, at first slowly and then with irregular vengeance. It seems to them, cradled inside, that the light is both coming closer and getting farther away as the boat fills with water. They only know it's water because the cold has soaked through their clothing and is beginning to penetrate skin. For the young ones, water has already chilled the bone, causing them to shake. Soon every scream will become pockets of escaped air. Soon water will fill every lung, stretching each to the limit.

Soon the sea will be calm.

For now, my father must try everything to stay alive. His panicked mind brings him to a childhood memory of falling off a bicycle for the first time, scraping both knees; how his mother scolded him before gently rubbing ointment on his injuries. His final thought as waves of darkness wash over him is regret for not knowing the future and what that future will do to the people he loves.

THE NEXT MORNING, A THAI fisherman out gathering drying nets sees debris scattered across the beach. He comes closer and makes out a shoe, a lighter, a flashlight. Torn pieces of cloth and fragments of wood. He picks up the shoe, which is miraculously in good condition, and attempts to find its pair.

This isn't the first wreckage he's seen. In the last few years, this scene on the beach has become a regularity. Once, a friend of his even found a tael of gold in a woven handbag, and this was when they realized someone else's misfortune could be their benefit. It's not uncommon to see fishermen and young children combing the beach in the morning after a storm.

The fisherman walks farther along the stretch of rocky sand, but the other shoe does not appear. Defeated, he chucks the one he's holding, and it lands next to a piece of paper wedged between some weeds. Curious, the fisherman comes closer to inspect and sees that it's a warped photograph of a family: a man standing next to a woman, and in front of them their children, two girls and two boys. Picking it up, the fisherman cannot know that this is my family—that taking photos at Turtle Lake every year, when spring arrives, was our tradition.

When he's done looking, the fisherman drops the photograph and walks back into his own life, leaving the picture to disintegrate slowly under the sun or be swept back into the salty sea.

Part III

WHAT MIGHT HAVE BEEN

10

THE LAST EMPEROR

MY FATHER LOST AT SEA.

This was where my made-up history reached its end, because what more is there to write after my father goes missing?
I took the circuitous route to reach the conclusion I have known
from the beginning—that he was dead.

All my words amounted to the same thing. No matter how
hard I tried, how far my imagination extended, I would never
have answers to what happened to him. I would continue to
wade in the cloudy waters of uncertainty. The story of my
father's absence arrived at its logical conclusion, so I stopped
writing and let living resume.

• • •

One spring afternoon, while clearing out the piles of paper that had accumulated on my desk, I found a strange image of geometric shapes in various shades of grey. It took me a moment to figure out that this was a Google Maps location of Phanat Nikhom. I'd printed it out years ago when I was gripped by the idea of returning to the refugee camp.

I held the wrinkled piece of paper and traced with my index finger the inverted-drop pin indicating the camp's location.

I realized then that I hadn't yet arrived at the end of the story I needed to create for myself. Even though my father was gone, we—my mother, my siblings, and I—were still here. And an emotional resolution was missing. I had to return to the refugee camp, where the life I led now first began, to see if I could figure out what I had felt then and unlock what I was feeling now, access another layer of my relationship to my father's ending. A physical return seemed like the final piece. Finding Phanat Nikhom became necessary.

This time, the idea of going back took on a propulsive quality. Finding the camp seemed entirely possible—buy a ticket, board an airplane, get inside a car, drive through the country roads, and arrive at the end.

So, I began planning methodically. I mapped out the upcoming year: how each month would be spent, where savings could be made, where to get visas and yellow-fever shots, when to leave, and the best month to stay. I was determined to make my return to the camp happen this time.

And it seemed the stars were aligning. I had a sabbatical on the way, which would release me from my teaching duties and allow me to travel out of the country. I had just recently entered middle age, and this trip to the refugee camp might allow me to start a new chapter in my life, however clichéd that seemed. Returning to the place where my new life had begun would be a renewal of sorts, I thought.

But to find the refugee camp, I would first have to arrive in Vietnam, where the journey had started. I considered retracing our family's successful—and my father's failed—migration route. I would take a bus from Ho Chi Minh City to Tây Ninh, then another bus to cross the Cambodian border into Phnom Penh. After that, I would find my way to Sihanoukville, not to bask in the golden sun on pristine beaches, but to travel farther into the swamps of Kampong Som bay. From there, I'd procure a boat and sail to Thailand.

I wondered what new knowledge I'd gain from following my family's migration journey. I wondered how it would alter me.

But I was hoping for too much again, getting far ahead of myself. I still hadn't found the exact location of Phanat Nik-hom, and nothing about my trip was guaranteed. I figured that sticking to a place I knew for sure was still there—Ho Chi Minh City—was where I should, indeed must, begin my return.

• • •

ONE EVENING, I WAS LOOKING into accommodations for Ho Chi Minh City and came across a listing for the historic Rex Hotel.

During the Vietnam War, the hotel was a hot spot for military personnel and international journalists. In the rooftop garden, the Americans held daily press briefings, which were derisively deemed "The Five O'Clock Follies" for the way they spun half-truths into reality, twisted facts to tell a winning story. Now the Rex was a luxury, five-star hotel at the centre of the city, housing stores like Chanel, Rolex, and Cartier, welcoming tourists with money to spend.

I was not going to stay at the Rex, but seeing the listing reminded me of an important piece of information a cousin had told me when we were in Texas for the family reunion. I had filed it away in a corner of my mind, but now it came flashing back with urgency.

We were sitting in a Chinese restaurant, enjoying a family banquet on our last night in Houston. My cousin, a couple of seats away, leaned over plates filled with stir-fried chicken and creamy lobster, and asked me, "Do you know what the last film Uncle Cẩn saw was?"

"What?" I almost screamed over the cacophony of chatter and laughter.

"Guess," he said with a mischievous smile.

I furrowed my eyebrows, then named a film I can no longer recall.

"It was *The Last Emperor*," he divulged.

"*The Last Emperor?*"

"He took me with him. We saw it at the Rex."

"The Rex Hotel?"

"Yes. It used to have a theatre."

"I didn't know."

"It was a week before he left—"

Then someone must have said something like, *Eat more of this delicious jellyfish before it's all gone*, or, *Do you want another Heineken?* or, *When are we all meeting up again?* because our exchange ended.

And that was that—the title of a film by Bernardo Bertolucci said aloud, the fact of my father having watched it at the Rex.

My imagination, like a director, started splicing scenes together to form a montage that began with a man entering a theatre to watch his final film. A single piece of information—something that would have been so unremarkable and insignificant to someone who had the good fortune of spending many years with their father—expanded for me into a two-hour-and-forty-three-minute epic.

I began writing once more. I was compelled to write about my father watching *The Last Emperor* because I thought it might illuminate something about how he had lived. I wouldn't write only about his death, but also about what could have been.

All the things that might have come to pass, the possible futures and alternate endings. A parallel, subjunctive world that is just as real as the one I had to stay in.

I decided I would write about his life, or, more precisely, his *living*. I'd imagine what I didn't know into existence, as I did in my made-up history. Writing how my father had lived, how he might have lived, how I wanted him to have lived, gave me a sense of control, which was the next best thing to having answers.

So, I found myself migrating through the fog of what might have been.

MY FATHER RUNS HIS LONG fingers through his hair. Then he does it again.

The last of the pomade his youngest brother sent from America sticks to his palm. The pomade is one of the only pleasures he has left, one of the few things that makes him feel human.

He looks into the small, rusty mirror hanging on the wall, which reflects only a fraction of his face, and sees a fragment of a man who's already left. This man looks like him, but only in form. The essence has escaped the bony face with deep lines crawling across the forehead; ridges that bracket the mouth; eyes so sunken they bulge forward; a long, sharp nose. The essence is in another country, looking for the refugee camp keeping his wife and children safe.

As my father buttons his shirt, a bead of sweat drips down the hollow of his collarbone. The heat this year has been unusually intense. He's looking forward to feeling the cool air conditioning.

He is on his way to see a film.

Cutting through the living room of his sister's house, where he stayed the night, my father passes her son, a teenager sitting in front of a small electric fan reading a book. He is shirtless, and my father sees the notches of his bent spine.

At the entrance, my father slips his feet into dusty sandals and readjusts one of the buckles. He thinks the sandals are too worn out, not adequate for the upcoming journey.

When he flips the kickstand of his bicycle, my father realizes he doesn't want to watch the film alone. He calls out his nephew's name and the teenager comes running. At the doorway, his nephew nods enthusiastically, glad to be released from studying for the afternoon and to escape the punishing heat.

My father leans against the bicycle and lights a cigarette as his nephew goes to grab a shirt. He thinks about the first film his father took him to see in Hanoi—Alfred Hitchcock's *To Catch a Thief*. What he remembers is a shadow falling over a seawall into the water, a man desperately trying to prove his innocence. It was the first time he saw colour on screen. Vietnamese words coming out of American mouths. My father takes a final drag of the cigarette and remembers the small hips of a woman he once loved, how youth did not last long for him.

His nephew returns and jumps on the bike's rear rack. Sitting hunched and saddled, his feet are barely above the ground. He puts his hands on my father's shoulders for balance, and together they take off. My father pedalling. His nephew trying to make himself lighter.

As they pass through concrete houses not yet rebuilt, my father wonders what great Hollywood films he will watch in the United States. He wonders how many years it will take for him to understand the dialogue without subtitles. He wonders whether his nephew's father, who migrated to New York alone years ago, working tirelessly to reunite their family, has the time to see movies.

My father's nephew wraps both arms tightly around his torso.

My father smiles.

They reach Nguyễn Huệ Street, which had once been a canal leading to the Saigon River before the French filled it to form a central boulevard. Riding down the street, they both feel the eerie sensation of floating on water.

They dock in front of the Rex Hotel. The building's brutalist facade, which hides its art-deco origins, rises six storeys high and converges on a corner intersection like an opened pair of wings. The building is painted a colonial pastel yellow, and the words REX HOTEL sit above two rows of red stars.

My father locks his bicycle, and they enter the building. When they reach the ticket counter, my father holds up his index and middle fingers, two for *The Last Emperor*.

They find good seats in the middle of the cool cinema. The late afternoon matinee is usually empty, except for a small scattering of lonely souls.

My father's nephew holds a large box of popcorn sprinkled with salt. He tells himself he will eat one kernel at a time, savouring each bite until the end credits roll.

My father lights a cigarette; its tip burns a brilliant orange in the dark. His mind wanders to the past, where he thinks about all the decisions he should have made. His life, he realizes, is full of missed opportunities—so many things he could have done differently.

Waiting for the film to start, my father wonders if the application he submitted years ago to relocate to the United States might actually come through.

His mind moves to the future. What if the approval arrives and he won't have to escape to Thailand next week? What if he immigrates to the United States before his wife and children? What if he could sponsor them? What if his bad fortune changes?

Then the screen lights up with the sound of beating drums, and my father enters into someone else's dream. He is transported to Manchuria in 1950, where Puyi, China's last emperor turned civilian, is being brought to a re-education prison run by the newly established Chinese Communist government. In the waiting area, Puyi attempts to take his own life by slitting his wrists. Red blood spreads in a basin of steaming water.

My father is shocked to see his own experience projected on the screen. Like the last emperor, he's been deemed an enemy of the state. He's been taken to prison too, he too has contemplated ending it all.

He doesn't like that film captures life in such cruel ways.

Then the magnificent Forbidden City appears onscreen. The most brilliant golds and reds fill every corner. For over an hour, ornate buildings and majestic robes, ceremonies and worldly opulence, provide a visual feast for his eyes. My father can't believe what he sees in front of him. A world like this exists, he marvels?

But then he understands that Puyi was a prisoner in the Forbidden City too. Puyi can't leave its gates. Even if you're the son of heaven, with everyone at your beck and call, you're still just an overstuffed rat stuck in a gilded cage.

Why is it so hard to escape one's life? he wonders.

He turns his attention back to the film in time to watch Puyi being forced into a confession, interrogated into rewriting his past life to suit the politics of the present.

My father feels a chill shoot through his body. He shakes tensely for a split second, as if his insides are rattling the bars of his rib cage, trying to break loose.

His nephew turns to him and says his name, Bac Cẩn.

On the screen in front of them, an interrogator tells Puyi that his confession and that of his valet do not match. Two stories can't be true at the same time. Facts must align. The interrogator throws the written confessions at Puyi's face.

My father thinks he can't possibly continue watching. But he tells himself this is only a film. It's not real. Nothing about the life he's lived feels real.

He lights another cigarette and settles down. He looks ahead at the screen but does not see what's in front of him— just a blur of light and moving shadows. My father only understands that it's the end when Puyi is freed into the life of an ordinary gardener, living quietly into old age. And then the lights come on.

My father's nephew is delighted. He's just seen the most incredible film, one that he will learn much later, as an American college student, won nine Oscars, including Best Picture. Imperial China stirs his imagination. Communist China makes him fear reality. He hasn't finished his popcorn and will bring what's left home to share with his brothers.

My father and his nephew exit the Rex when the sun is about to disappear completely. The city is lit up in the most vibrant hues of orange and pink. It is one of those dusks when Saigon looks as if it's on fire, the inhabitants burning brightly as they move about their ordinary lives—walking down the street, hawking bowls of steaming soup, waving someone goodbye.

Men on rusty cyclos call out to them, asking if they need a ride on ancient-looking three-wheeled rickshaws. Motorbikes whiz by, honking as my father and his nephew cross the street to unlock the bicycle.

My father tells his nephew to hang on tight while he pedals with abandon down the wide boulevard. The evening breeze tousles their hair. It lashes their faces as they speed up. They are going so fast that their eyes squint to see. Then they take a sudden turn, disappearing into a labyrinth of alleys, the film still lingering somewhere in both their minds.

As SOON AS I FINISHED imagining my father watching *The Last Emperor*, I began packing my suitcase.

11

DECISION TO LEAVE

I'M SURROUNDED BY HANDBAGS MADE in China. Faux leather and fake gold chains reflected in the shop's mirrors, an infinity room of purses. Women are sizing up and trying on merchandise, helped by enthusiastic staff my cousin employs. This is the cousin who's the same age as me, the only cousin who still lives in Vietnam. She and I sit facing each other as the AC blasts freezing air over our exposed limbs. The sun outside glares through the window.

I haven't seen this cousin in many years. The last time we were together, my grandmother was still alive, and I came into the house asking to see photo albums. We were both in our twenties then. Now, a little more grown, we embrace and exchange pleasantries. There's a lot of catching up to do between us, a lot of selfies to take and send to family members who live far away.

I marvel at our resemblance—the long, round face; the thick, dark hair; the sad, watery eyes. Others will remark that we are exactly like brother and sister when they see us together. We let the words come and go as they please. I stumble over the threshold of my Vietnamese. People enter and exit our conversations. The past loops back, and then the present reasserts itself. We chat, in a corner of the shop, like two people who have the luxury of a full day to themselves. We get to know each other again in a changed Ho Chi Minh City.

The conversation eventually comes around to my father, her uncle. She's forgotten much about him. When he left, and why. She no longer remembers that my family and I spent three years in refugee camps.

"Why didn't the whole family leave together?" she asks. "Why separate?"

I don't know how to explain a decision other people made. I don't know how to explain something I wish were different.

A logical answer does not make sense here.

I know that my mother gave my father the choice: either he takes the children or she does, but they both agreed that it was wiser not to go as a whole family. On the chance that we all die, or are captured and returned, or the smuggle was a scam. So my father stayed and waited. He held on to our house and our old life.

My father was to follow after us, embark on the same route. He was supposed to depart when he received news, through a letter from my mother or word from the smugglers, that we had arrived. The plan was already mapped out for him.

All this information seems inadequate. It explains nothing.

When he received news that we were safe, he must have hurried to the smuggler to secure his place on the next boat out. A path had finally opened up for him.

And yet he waited.

Because something else beyond him and our family had been brewing. It was called HO—*hat oh*—or Humanitarian Operation.

As postwar boat refugees, in the hundreds of thousands, arrived on the shores of neighbouring countries, world leaders converged on Geneva in 1979 to solve the problem, putting words on paper that would change people's fates. Conferences with important men produced reams of memoranda and reports. Policies were signed. They wanted emigration to be more *orderly*, for *departures* to be firmly controlled in the hands of government officials.

No more boats, they all agreed.

And my father's seven-year re-education gave him a ticket into this new program.

He submitted an application.

He waited. And waited.

He knew painfully well how bureaucracy worked. There were whispers of delays and cancellations. There was fear the program would be suspended. Unexplainable denials. Many people being hung from the neck with red tape.

But in the back of his mind, he also wondered, *What if?* What if a miracle came through, and the impossible happened? He could, at some auspicious moment, get the approval to leave—a coveted visa.

What he has to do, what he does, is all a matter of speculation. If he leaves, we risk losing everything we have: our house, our possessions, our life we were willing to leave behind—that life was better than no life at all. If he leaves, he puts himself in the mouth of danger. If he stays, he might receive an envelope with a positive reply and a ticket to America. From there he could sponsor us in the camp. If he stays just a little longer, his luck might change. If he stays, he may no longer have a heart to break. If he leaves right away, he'll be able to place his lips on his wife's forehead, and let his youngest child straddle his torso. They will all sleep in one room again. If he leaves, he takes his life in his own hands. If he stays, his life is protected for another day.

I tell my cousin simply that he stayed to keep our house from being confiscated.

She makes a noise that acknowledges my answer.

"Such a waste," she says.

I nod. And before I even know what I'm saying, I add: "Now there is no life and no house also."

•   •   •

My father makes a decision.

How much waiting is too much waiting? my father thinks to himself as he walks his bicycle down a small alley. A light breeze passes through the worn cotton of his white shirt, and this may have given him reprieve from the decision, a moment when it did not poke at his ribs. He moves in the balmy night without haste, a man with no place to be.

He is of two minds. This or that. To stay or to go? What will be?

My father has just left his mother's house, where she and his younger sister pleaded with him not to leave. "Just sit tight," they said. "Be patient, your time will come. You've waited this long, what's there to lose in holding still a bit longer?"

But he sighed, "How much can one man endure?"

And they saw the suffering in his eyes. A man anchored and adrift at the same time. They knew he was an animal in a cage, held captive in his own life for far too long.

So, they did not press him. They sent him home, with an appeal to think things over.

But he walks a path that does not lead back to his house, and he does not notice where it takes him.

As he walks, the leaves above him rustle into the city's void. Closer to the ground, a voice calls out to those who hunger, hanging on to the final waking hours. The night is alive with shadows.

My father walks until, suddenly, he realizes he's reached Turtle Lake, its octagonal shape hidden by the dark. Squinting, he makes out some steps and the tower that blooms at the top.

He sits down on a bench and grins.

This is the place he's been looking for all along.

He remembers every family photo taken here.

Then the blur of a little boy flashes across my father's eyes. For a split second he thinks he recognizes this boy as his very own. He extends his arm, but it finds only empty space.

My father would believe he's imagined the boy if not for the mother who follows behind, imploring her son to slow down. He hears a small giggle and footsteps echoing in the dark.

In this moment, something irreversible happens. He waits until the boy and his mother circle around again. The night has become even darker. My father stands up, gets on his bicycle, and pedals slowly into a street being swallowed by cruelty.

He makes a decision.

My father made a decision.

This is what I think to myself decades removed from the event. I know he wanted to make the right decision. For a long time, I couldn't comprehend what the right decision would have been, or if there was one. And now, I think the right decision was not so much about outcome, but more its ability to give my father a pardon, to make things less complicated for a man already buried under two lifetimes' worth of unmercies. In my middle age, I think I understand my father's inability to bear all this uncertainty on his shoulders.

He was aware something would be lost. He decided to give up the house, but he didn't know that wasn't enough. He would need to exchange more. The final price would be that we'd live a life without him.

MY FATHER LEAVES.

He takes only a small cloth bag of his belongings, as he was instructed to do: all that he has to his name in the form of gold, the currency of those without a country, and one photograph of our family.

Under the cover of darkness, he makes his way to the meeting point. His heart races. He's terrified of what's to come, of the unknown and the unknowable, the fate that waits for him by the shore.

He sits in the hold of a truck with other hopeful souls and thinks of his mother. He is filled with regret.

A month earlier, when he had told her of his decision to leave, she responded with a mother's last resort: guilt. She wanted so desperately for him to stay that she called him unfilial. In his frustration he blurted out that he needed to live his own life, that he was a husband and father too.

"HE SAID THAT?" I ASK my cousin.

She nods. "He did."

There was no returning from the decision.

Before my cousin told me of this final rift between my father and his mother, I didn't think his leaving could have been worse, could have had more tragedy.

If she were still alive, I could have made repairs in his place, could've told his mother that he made the wrong decision, that he should have stayed with her.

Knowing often comes too late.

So, a silence cleft between my father and his mother like a stubborn splinter, and neither of them tried to dislodge it, waiting for the other to make the first move.

Both would wait forever.

THE NIGHT BEFORE HE LEAVES, he walks past her house one last time, but he does not go in.

Instead of asking his mother for forgiveness, he walks the small alleys that crawl through the city like tunnels on the verge of crumbling onto themselves. He is a departed ghost making his way toward the beginning of the end. He's so full of feeling that he can no longer separate hope from despair, longing from dread. He is a man, among millions of other men, walking away.

My father makes his decision. And it pivots our lives in irrevocable ways. It sends us in directions not of our own choosing. We are the ones who have to live out his final decision. There is no right or wrong, just long-lasting repercussions. So I excavate his decision. I construct word memorials around it.

• • •

A CUSTOMER ENTERS THE SHOP looking for a green shoulder bag and my cousin turns to help her, while I sit back in disbelief that I'm actually in Vietnam. It's difficult for me to accept that my feet are planted on soil made from memories interspersed with bones of the war dead. This country is a graveyard, I think.

Who am I and what am I doing here?

What is it that I want from this place?

When my cousin calls my name, I snap out of my reverie. I feel my shivering body, frozen from the blasting AC.

"It's such a waste," she says again.

"If only he had waited." She looks right at me.

"What difference would that have made?" I ask.

She pauses and doesn't answer.

MY GRANDMOTHER WAKES IN THE early hours of the morning, when the crowing of roosters gives way to the call of alley hawkers. Something has come over her—a premonition, intuition, dread. She locates it in the place where her throat becomes her chest. In the years to come she'll know that this is something only a mother can feel. A pain not of your body, but you still must carry it as your own. It's like dying, but your eyes open every morning.

She gets up, gathers the mosquito net, and ties it into a big knot above her mattress, before doing the same thing to her once-ebony-black hair, which is now streaked with grey.

Without the aid of electricity, she descends the flight of stairs and enters the kitchen in the dark. She hears two rats convening in tiny voices, deciding whether they should leave, and she stamps her foot twice against the cool earth. They scurry away, and she is alone.

The bruised blue of dawn seeps through a window and crawls toward the kitchen, where my grandmother is scooping rainwater from a cistern into a washing bowl. She gently brings the water to her face in the same spot where she will continue to cook meals for those who come back to visit, until illness confines her to a cot in the front room. It is here that her eldest daughter, who left for New York, will hold her and they will both cry, knowing that no words need be exchanged because words do nothing good in lives like theirs. It is here that she will pass on her recipes to the only grandchild who still lives by her side. It is here that she will, one day, suddenly, wonder what her eldest son's children are like, whether they know their father the way she knows her son. She will wonder if it's cold where these grandchildren are and if they remember who she is.

She smooths the brown pajama tunic against her bony body and slips the only beautiful thing she has left—a jade bracelet—onto her wrist. She prepares the plastic carrier and enters the newly arrived day, heading to the wet market down the road. She knows that those who arrive early get the best produce. She knows that sellers wanting to unblock the flow of good luck will lower prices for the first customer.

The market is already alive, even at this early hour. And by the time she bumps into a neighbour, it's teeming with people.

My grandmother and her neighbour embrace and exchange tips about where to get the freshest picks this morning.

In a couple of decades, tourists wearing conical hats will stumble into or seek out this place, hoping for an authentic picture of Vietnam. They will point their giant lenses at shallots and starfruit, catfish and cilantro, asking women to smile without realizing that the entire market runs on the fuel of mourning. The shadows lurking in their vacation photos are those who've disappeared.

This morning, my grandmother decides she will braise pork with a touch of anise. She asks for the thickest cut of belly. The butcher gives her a price, and she throws another one back. A new one is given, and a counter-offer is returned. They both budge and give while holding ground. They both know that a few dongs is still a saving. This is not their first dance, nor their last. They are, in the end, friends.

Once my grandmother agrees, the butcher wraps the meat in old newspaper while telling her that she's made no profit with the sale. My grandmother says she's blown her budget with this one luxury. They both thank each other, smiling with their teeth.

While she heads off with her pork belly, a mailman is waiting at the door for my grandmother. He has a bag over his shoulders, and this bag holds bundles of letters. He knocks on the door, but no one answers. He knocks again and decides to smoke a cigarette. He takes his time to savour the bitter tobacco.

As he stubs out his cigarette and gets on his bicycle to continue the morning's round, my grandmother turns the corner. She sees him and waves her free hand. She hurries toward him.

He greets her and hands her an envelope.

It's addressed to her eldest son, who left her a month ago, whom she hasn't heard from since his last coded letter informing her that he'd made it to Cambodia.

She stands still for a moment. She doesn't remember thanking the mailman or him leaving.

She enters her house, and the first thing she does is open the letter with her wrinkled, trembling fingers.

There is official letterhead. There is a salutation. There is an invitation. She registers none of this and will only understand later, when she asks her daughter to read the letter for her and confirm that her son's HO application was successful. He is invited to bring his family to a formal interview, after which he will receive a visa to come to the United States.

My cousin tells me this crucial piece of information, and I let out a gasp.

My grandmother drops the letter and lets out a sharp, muted scream.

She does not notice that on the floor, where her morning haul lies, the newspaper wrapping has opened, like a blooming flower, revealing the meat inside, or that a fly has already found its way there, landing on sweet, sweet flesh.

12

A NEW LIFE BEGINS

My FATHER PULLS OPEN THE metal gate, and it contracts like an accordion, revealing the mailman holding an envelope.

Before it's fully in his hands, my father rips the envelope open and, with hasty fingers, unfolds the letter, which blooms with all the beauty of the climbing bougainvillea in a pot on the balcony above him. This is the only plant that remains alive in the house. He'd given up, had already begun to leave this place behind in his mind. But the bougainvillea is resilient. It survives without his attention, on shafts of afternoon sun and fallen rainwater. My father begins to read:

Mr. Nguyễn Ngọc Cẩn:

We have reviewed your application and invite you to an interview at our office. Your eligibility for the Humanitarian Operation subprogram is conditional on this interview, and the subsequent evidence you submit to substantiate your case . . .

He skims the rest and sees a date, an address, and a signature in blue ink. The signature gives him hope that this letter might not be a cruel joke, might not be another ruse to imprison him. He reads the letter once more to make sure it really says what he thinks it says. Everything he has experienced in the past decade has hammered doubt into his head. What he knows cannot be trusted. What he sees might not be real. What he touches disappears.

After what seems like a lifetime elapsing on a thin piece of paper, my father lets out a cry of relief. His voice echoes down the tiny alley as he hugs the man delivering this good news. "I can go. I can go now."

A neighbour peeks around the corner and sees two aging men patting each other on the back, so jubilant they almost float off the ground together.

My father barely gets the gate closed before he's on his bicycle, pedalling like a man finally unlatched from his own life, the back strap of his leather sandals flattened and twisted beneath his calloused heels. On the way to his mother's house, he composes a letter in his mind:

My beloved wife—

Our reunion is coming. Just this morning, I received the let-
ter that contains the answer we've been waiting for. I can't
believe this is happening, but next month I will meet with
the Americans. If everything is in order, they will grant me
asylum. We've agonized for so long, but everything seems to
be speeding up now. I must work hard to ensure nothing goes
wrong. There isn't enough time. I never stop thinking of you
and the children. Continue to love life. Until we meet again.

Your devoted husband,
Căn

My father can't stop grinning as he weaves his bicycle
through the clogged Saigon streets, his muscles taut, his lean
figure a lightning rod conducting a new future for us all. He
narrowly misses plowing into a group of men on the sidewalk,
huddled on red plastic stools, slurping steaming bowls of soup
to begin the day. He turns a corner and then another, moving
by instinct because the familiar city no longer looks the way
it should. Everything he sees is in the process of evaporating
from his life. He's so alive he does not feel the drizzle that soaks
through the white shirt clinging to his chest.

My father lives.

• • •

WHEN HIS PAPERS ARRIVE, HE transfers the deed of our house over to his sister. He no longer has a use for it. My father promises he will sponsor the entire family when he is settled. He now believes that there is no end to hope. He shops for new outfits because he doesn't know whether American clothes will fit him, or whether he will look good in them. He wants to be presentable wherever he ends up. He wants everything to be fresh. What he owns, which isn't much, he exchanges for flat sheets of gold, to be sewn into the seams of his pants' waist.

In his final days in Vietnam, he indulges with his buddies. They drink cheap beer and whisky, pass out, wake up, and drink some more; they dare the night to end, lighting cigarette after cigarette for each other; they stumble home singing the saddest of songs as dawn approaches.

Then, before he knows it, he is crying at Tân Sơn Nhất Airport, telling his mother and siblings that this is not goodbye but see you soon. He boards an airplane, which takes him to a small island in the Pacific Ocean, where he spends the night before getting on a larger airplane bound for California. It is his first time outside Vietnam.

He arrives at the San Diego International Airport, where military jeeps are waiting to transfer him and other Vietnamese refugees to Camp Pendleton, where they are processed as new arrivals. In the camp, he uses the little English he picked up during his time in the military; he takes every opportunity to strike up broken conversations with the marines, asking for a smoke, asking about the weather, asking what life outside the barracks will be like.

On the day he leaves Pendleton, the Southern California desert is scorching hot. As he steps outside the camp's gates, squinting to see the road ahead, he remembers another moment of freedom and chuckles at these strange rebirths for a man who wasn't supposed to live. He takes an uncertain step forward, his new life tightly packed in a grey suitcase, bound for a city called San Jose, where a thriving community of Vietnamese refugees have been attempting to rebuild a facsimile of their homeland.

In his first letter to us from the United States, he describes the tiny apartment he shares with two other men, how there are cockroaches but no rats like there were in Vietnam. He tells us he's been painting houses with these men, how a white van picks them up in the morning whenever there's work and they are paid in green bills at the end of the day. He says that Americans want their walls white, pure, and clean without traces of the people who live or have lived within them. He tells us he will—must—make it in this new country. He tells us that he misses us. That he is happy.

He spends countless mornings and afternoons speaking to people at resettlement services and filling out forms, making sure that anyone who cares to know knows he has a family currently stuck in a refugee camp.

We remain patient. My mother requests multiple appointments with UN officers, telling them that we want to go to the United States. It can only be the United States, because we have a life waiting for us there.

My father continues to send letters, and we respond with our own hopeful ones; my mother knows that men like him require tender encouragement. She sends him photos of us dressed up and posing our optimism for him. He tells her how beautiful she looks, how every child has grown so much in his absence, how the little one twisting his skinny legs, holding a blond Barbie, makes him smile.

He sends a photograph of himself standing in front of a large strip mall, next to four statues. There are three in the back: the first is a long-bearded sage holding a peach in one hand and a staff in the other, representing longevity; the second is a mandarin holding a child, representing happiness; and the third is an official carrying a giant tael of gold with both hands, representing prosperity. A pot-bellied Buddha sits in the front. The statues are all smiling, but my father has the biggest grin in the image.

A year and two months after he sends us this photograph, we walk through the arrivals gate of San Jose Mineta International Airport and into his open arms. These arms stretch wide, bridging the distance that had opened up, drawing all the fallen bits and pieces, us his family, together again.

Through her tears, my mother sees his face for the first time in many years. She reaches to touch his cheekbones, which, while always high, have become more pronounced. The shape of his face has changed; it's longer now and emptied of youthful flesh and more prosperous times. Someone who doesn't love him would describe it as gaunt. His dark skin stretched tight over bones, but deep lines have set in around his eyes and on his forehead. As he stares back at her, she sees tired eyes behind the spark of his expressive grin. The only thing that hasn't changed is the row of straight teeth, yellowed by tobacco, peeking out from his full brown lips.

She thinks to herself, This is my husband. But the thought sounds more like a loving question.

WHAT WE BEGIN IS A life together. This is the life of a full and complete family: father, mother, two daughters, and two sons. We all squeeze into a one-bedroom apartment, and just like in Vietnam, we lay two mattresses on the floor in the living room and sleep side by side.

Our first few months in this new life, it seems that we do everything with and for one another. We stick close when we stroll the neighbourhood, peering into the opened windows of houses to glimpse what might become possible. We sit in a row at the stuffy welfare office. We move in a line down the supermarket aisle. We ride the city bus to school together. We raise bowls of phở to our mouths at the same table. We hold hands while waiting for my father to pass his driving test. And, like this, time passes, and we settle into a kind of American routine.

My father gets a new job shortly after we arrive. This one is more stable than painting walls. He wakes up every morning at four thirty, when the sky is still black, and smokes a cigarette. Its orange tip glows in the dark, illuminating the contours of his face when he pulls a drag. This is the only time he gets to be alone with his thoughts. He thinks how odd it is for him to be standing on the landing of an American apartment building, how he can hear the indistinct sounds of his native language floating up from the floor below, how one thing could never fit with another, but it's not up to him. He wants this third chance to work out, wants to live like a man grabbing freedom by the throat, forcing it to yield its promised fruits. He knows that it will take many mornings, and that he is ready.

My mother wakes up every morning just after him and puts the kettle on. She mixes Nescafé together with Coffee-mate and sugar in a cup. When she adds water, clumps of brown-and-white powder bubble to the top. The spoon she uses to dissolve these clumps makes clinking sounds. And as if on cue, my father enters the kitchen and downs the hot coffee in three large gulps. He grabs the plastic bag she hands him, containing his lunch, kisses her on the cheek, smiles, and slips out the door before any of his children is awake. He gets into a used Ford Tempo and drives along stretches of freeway while the rest of the city sleeps.

When he arrives at the factory, the morning light is just beginning to descend on the concrete structure, giving it a rosy-golden sheen, a fleeting beauty that escapes perception if one does not pause to look. My father and those like him pass unaware through the factory's open doors. Inside, my father takes his station, where he's tasked with fitting small pieces of plastic onto what they call motherboards—square sheets of copper and fibreglass with intricate lines, numbers, and letters etched

on them, as well as ports, slots, and screw holes. Each motherboard, he thinks, looks like a glittering futuristic city.

He begins by grabbing a small plastic piece, which reminds
him of a red Monopoly house, with his left thumb and forefin-
ger while simultaneously using his right hand to slide a board
from a pile toward the left. As the two hands meet, the left low-
ers the piece over a raised metal rectangle, clicking it into place,
and the right slides the board onward into another pile. This
motion he repeats thousands and thousands of times throughout the day, stopping only for forty minutes when he eats the
rice with either pork or chicken and cabbage stir-fry my mother
has packed, and then inhales multiple cigarettes.

He does this Monday to Friday, and when the boss sees that
he's doing a good job and offers him overtime, my father starts
waking up at four thirty on Saturdays too. On Sundays, he's
exhausted, but he gathers the energy to drive us all to the Vietnamese grocery, where my mother buys her weekly supplies of
morning glory, pork belly, taro root, yellow chicken, and other
items too "ethnic" to be found anywhere else. When we're
done, we shuffle back into the car and head home, where my
mother prepares dinner while I roam the neighbourhood with
friends and my father cracks open beers with the neighbours in
the building's parking lot.

Sometimes these neighbours pile into our apartment, and
my mother lays newspaper out on the floor for the men to sit on
while they snack on "drinking food," crunchy pig ears and salty
peanuts, cuttlefish and cold cuts, shaken beef with watercress.

These sessions often last long into the night: the women gossip or trade recipes in the kitchen, my siblings play video games in the apartment next door, and I fall asleep in the corner of the living room, which fills with smoke as the men's boisterous and slurred voices echo through walls.

Once in a while, on very special occasions, my parents dress up to go listen to music at a community centre, where women with big hair, in sequined gowns, and men in flashy suits belt out old Vietnamese tunes to rapturous crowds of drunken refugee men and dolled-up refugee women. My parents cha-cha-cha and lambada on the dance floor; they lip-synch lyrics ingrained forever in their consciousness. Late in the night, my father caresses my mother's arm and holds her by the waist, pulling her onto his lap. She kisses the forehead of his red, glowing face and whispers, "I adore you," as the strobe lights and smoke machine prolong their dream world for another hour.

Back at work, my father is promoted to the role of solderer after just a year on the job. He holds a pen-like instrument that releases hot metal when it touches the motherboard, fusing one thing to another. He makes $1.50 more per hour. But just four months after his promotion, the factory shuts down and my father is laid off.

While my mother attends vocational college in the daytime to earn her GED, my father takes me to school and then asks around for work. In the mid-afternoon, he waits for me at the bus stop. Sometimes we go to the park near our apartment, where I play on the swings, go down the slide, and hang on monkey bars while he sits and smokes. Sometimes he takes me to the café where men like him hang out. They discuss work prospects, families back in Vietnam, and ways to leave the city. They sip coffee, smoke, and laugh, patting each other on the back. I entertain a sweet bowl of vanilla ice cream with crushed peanuts sprinkled on top, listen, and learn.

During this period, my father works construction for a few months. He goes back to painting walls on and off. He helps his friend out at a restaurant, busing tables during the lunch rush. He works in a warehouse loading boxes onto trucks. He considers learning a trade—electrician, plumber, mechanic. He takes the graveyard shift as a security guard.

Then he receives a letter from someone he trained with decades ago in the South Vietnamese army. There is work in Texas, it says. He makes the decision to move the family to Houston to take a job at a slaughterhouse, trimming cow carcasses. My mother is not happy with the decision, but she does not push back because she's seen how much he's put into willing this new life for us. She does not want him to get discouraged and give up. She knows we can make it work in any city, as long as we're together.

In Houston, we start over again. We live in a duplex with two bedrooms. My sisters share one room while my parents and I share the other. My brother sleeps on the couch. It's what he wants, some privacy. Our neighbourhood is poor, populated by mostly Black and brown families who speak Spanish and drawling English. We make friends, for the first time, with non-Vietnamese people. We also fight with them, believing the stories we see on TV, confirmed by first-hand experience of mundane strife. We become more and more American every day.

Because he has to hack dead animals into parts, because he sees so much blood and smells so much death, my father makes sure to be extra tender to his wife and children. At home he never raises his voice. When my parents argue, they do so in whispers late in the night or boxed in the car. My father lets my mother have her way, always. I learn to use a bottle opener and to perform the part of a carefree and adoring son. His booming laughter, which undulates between deep bass and ecstatic shrill, fills the family with a sense of security.

He spends his best remaining work years, the strength he has left in his body, at the slaughterhouse. My father begins to understand that this is all that will open up for him in this new life. And he continues to wake up every morning.

My mother, with GED in hand, lands a job at a family doctor's office, where she keeps track of patient files and learns to use a computer. She makes friends with the women who work there, and they often have lunch dates to eat fat pieces of steak.

At first, it's just a few, sporadic nights, when my father drinks too much and falls asleep on the couch with my brother as the TV glares into the darkness. And then gradually this sleeping arrangement becomes permanent. My brother is upset, but there's nothing he can say, so he keeps silent and tolerates the twin mattress placed beneath the couch. When my father is not at work, he spends his time, his best remaining years, drinking with other Vietnamese men in cafés and pool halls.

My mother wants my father to quit smoking, to drink less, and stay at home more. When we take our first family trip, driving from Houston to New York City, where my father's sister has recently resettled, my mother does not speak a single word. We children sit in the back seat. My eldest sister fidgets with her yellow Walkman, my other sister and brother focus on their opened comic books, and I, in the middle, stare out the windshield at the moving cars ahead of us. My father lights one cigarette after another. And with his window rolled down, the ashes whip back into our faces.

My mother wants to migrate north to Canada, where her parents live, but my father wants to go east to New Orleans, where there are Vietnamese-owned companies with multiple shrimp trawlers. He thinks we can make a new start there, move up in life by going out to sea on a boat again.

We move, instead, back to California, this time closer to the San Francisco Bay. My mother works in the crowded kitchen of a popular Asian chain restaurant. She teaches the younger workers, mostly undocumented Mexicans, how to fold egg rolls so the ends are tight and even. She signs up for a twelve-week baking course on the weekends and comes home with practice pieces of cake to a delighted household. She learns, too, how to drive stick and manoeuvres her vehicle fearlessly around the city and across the Bay.

Something happens to my father upon this return to California. Perhaps he's had one too many do-overs, one too many lifetimes, but it is as if his worn tires are leaking air and the tired engine guzzles more fuel than it can handle. The Ford chugs along, releasing dark fumes into the air, and my father is a ghost of himself.

A family friend suggests he learn to do nails and find work at one of the many salons that dot every strip mall. He tells my father to come along with him and apprentice for a week, see what he thinks. My father, with his calloused fingers, which can no longer coordinate, so used now to holding instruments of death such as rifles or butcher knives, cannot adjust to a file or clippers, cannot stay inside the nail bed when he paints. The smell of toluene makes him nauseous. The customers leave dissatisfied, without getting the beauty they paid for.

When we fly to Calgary to visit my grandparents for the first time, it's the Christmas holidays. We come woefully underprepared for the cold, but my mother's parents and fourteen siblings greet us at the airport with extra scarves, gloves, and winter coats as if we were newly arrived refugees. My mother cries to her sisters when they are alone, telling them what a struggle it has been, how her husband has tried everything, how she holds them all together, and how her youngest sometimes drifts away to places she's afraid of.

We have a giant gathering at my grandparents' house, and my father goes outside to have a cigarette and then he disappears into the freezing night. My uncles get into cars and drive around the neighbourhood looking for him. Their headlights make fat beams through the falling snow.

Hours later, when my father shows up at the house again, his ears and nose are red, but his mood is jubilant. He reassures everyone that he just needed some fresh air, that he lost track of time. He pours more of the Hennessy he bought at the duty-free into everyone's glasses, and they all pretend nothing happened. The night is young and his laughter resounding, infectious. We never find out where he went or what he did for those missing hours.

We return to California full of family and regret, but also rejoicing at the warm breeze from the Pacific, at how our skins do not crack. And the sun, the shining sun. We all head back to our daily responsibilities. My father stays home to clean the apartment and learns to prepare dinner. He smokes a pack a day.

And then a phone call arrives from his youngest sister in Vietnam: "Brother Cẩn—Mother's health has been declining. She is weak and she calls for you. As the eldest in the family, you must come and be by her side. She needs you."

He buys a ticket to a country he's vowed never to step foot in again, not while the Communists are in power. Not while those who've made him suffer, his enemies who've destroyed his homeland, could benefit from his hard-earned American dollars.

But as the new millennium begins, five years after watching his president, Bill Clinton, announce that Hanoi had been co-operating with the United States to return the remains of those soldiers once declared missing in action, providing many American families with closure, my father returns to Saigon to visit his mother. What these politicians call diplomatic "normalization" has allowed many refugees like him to return home to see long-lost family.

He goes alone because we can't afford for all six members of the family to cross the Pacific Ocean.

At Tân Sơn Nhất Airport, he has to go through immigration, and the young officer—the smell of breast milk fresh in his mouth, as the saying goes—demands a bribe, five dollars for entry into the past. Already my father feels like a stranger coming back to someone else's future. Stepping outside the building, it's the intense tropical sun that hits him first, and this too feels like a new beginning. From the back window of a taxi, everything looks the same, but also it doesn't. He feels as though he hasn't changed, but the driver treats him differently, with both regard and suspicion.

He arrives home, and his mother is lying on a cot in the front room. When she hears him call out to her, she shifts her pelvis and turns her face toward the wall. My father begins making amends by touching her shoulder.

He gets on a borrowed bicycle and leisurely pedals to meet an old friend. They plan to relive an epic night of debauchery; they wish to rewind the clock with copious amounts of beer.

As the sun sets, and the city transitions, relieved from the day's heat, my father observes women serving food on the street and friends sipping beverages at corner stalls. He sees raisined men sleeping on parked cyclos beneath a tangle of wires carrying electricity from one pole to another, students with backpacks on their shoulders ambling home, and stray dogs rummaging through garbage. What enters his mind is the life he could have lived, what might have been if he had stayed.

My father composes a letter to my mother in his mind, but he knows it will never be sent. He continues pedalling the bicycle slowly into a foreclosed possibility.

When he goes through security and boards a plane to return to the life he chose with us, my father wonders if he'll ever return to Vietnam again. He thinks he wants to stay, but he's not sure what this feeling is that pulls him in different directions as the plane cuts through the atmosphere.

Back in California, my father starts a new job when he should be thinking of retirement. Like many enterprising refugees, he gave himself a later birthdate on all legal documents, knowing that youth is a prized possession for those facing reinvention. And with youth comes more precious years of work. What he didn't know was that these additional years would keep him from his hard-earned social security. That work in the land of opportunity would grind his body down low to the ground.

He wakes up every morning, gets out of bed, and stretches his stiff body, extending his fingers to the sky. My father looks like he's praying, as though he's making a quiet, ceremonious entreaty in the dark. Then he drags himself to the warehouse where he operates a forklift, moving large boxes containing things like three-door refrigerators and high-definition televisions from one corner to another. He carries smaller boxes by hand, bending over—his lower back supported by a brace underneath his shirt—to pick them up. With the force of his torso, he loads items onto and off delivery trucks. He organizes shelves, reaching his arms in one direction and then another to rearrange merchandise and make space. He uses a tattered broom to sweep the floor clean of dirt and debris.

The years, and the unremarkable things that happen to men like him, they pass.

He sits on an overturned, yellow plastic crate by the scratched-up, no-longer-white double doors at the back of the warehouse. My father smokes cigarettes with two immigrant workers, one Korean and the other Somalian. The Korean sits across from him, back bent, intently studying the pocket dictionary in his hand like a bible, while the Somalian leans against the wall, blowing at a Styrofoam cup. They are a trinity, three points of an imperfect triangle. Smoke curls and dissipates around them.

The Korean man's lips are moving. He makes a series of sounds, *ian-di-bee-chul*, at first slowly and then with more confidence, *indibechul*. "What it mean?"

My father takes the dictionary from him and reads, "A single human being as distinct from a group, class, or family." He points to the man, *you*, and then up to the other, *him*, and finally to himself, *me*. "We are individuals. A self. A person. *One*." He holds up a finger. "Not many. Not family."

The Korean puckers his mouth. "But how can be *indibechul* with no family?" he asks.

"No good, no good," he says, clicking his teeth, without requiring an answer.

They all understand what he means, and let out small, coarse chuckles.

Yes, it is no good, the trinity decrees.

A head squeezes out of the crack kept open by a wooden doorstop. "Time, come on."

My father takes one last drag of his cigarette and then crushes it to the ground.

The Korean closes his dictionary and stands up. The Somalian turns to pull the door wide open.

As they move, little drops of rain begin falling from the sky. Each man a free individual passing through the warehouse's threshold, all sharing one big dream.

13

KILL YOUR FATHER

"WHY DO YOU HAVE TO kill your father?" my partner asked as we tried to avoid the murky puddles at a side entrance of Trinity Bellwoods Park. It had been raining continuously for the past week, and I was emerging from the cocoon of my apartment for the first time in days. Above us, dark clouds gathered against a uniform grey, swallowing the top of the CN Tower, which rose in the skyline to the east.

My return trip—taken almost exactly half a year before— seemed far removed from this rain-soaked Toronto. Ho Chi Minh City and Bangkok, with their bright, scorching afternoons, felt like a different world. The crucial piece of information about my father's HO approval was already an evaporated memory.

I didn't know how to answer my partner. I stayed silent for a while, flipping through responses in my mind: he's not that lucky, I'm a cruel son, I'm obsessed with his death, history is inescapable, my imagination has limits. None of these answers actually get at the truth of my predicament, but all of them are true. We continued walking along the path that led us into the park.

I was, for the first time in my life, in charge of the death that had defined who I thought I was and how I related to the world around me. This was my chance to change the story and narrate what could have been as a way to better understand what was.

But I hadn't realized the repercussions of writing a counter-factual story of my father's death. On the page and in my mind, I had the agency to orchestrate an alternate journey for him, guide him through obstacles so he could avoid a premature death. Possessing this agency, however, did not make me feel powerful or invincible. It didn't bring resolution. What it did was appeal to my need for control, to believe, however illusory it might be, that I was not at the mercy of existential forces conspiring to knock me over at every turn. What it did was explode the story, and make anything and everything possible. It fractured his death into a million different questions.

Writing my father's could-have-been life dislodged me because it made me confront the mess of living. With his hypothetical survival, everything would have to be rearranged, the architecture of my family redrawn. The house needed more rooms. The furniture moved and moved again to make space. Our lives suspended, needing a complete rewrite. Perhaps that was the most difficult aspect of this exercise, to revise the lives that did unfold to accommodate the life that did not.

Who are we? How did we become who we are? And more importantly, what did we miss out on?

Considering the possibility that my mother, my siblings, and I could have had different lives had become too painful. I questioned whether I had the capacity to re-create our lives on the page. I questioned whether I was a good enough writer to open the floodgates. It seemed, all of a sudden, much simpler to put into words what I knew had happened, however limited that knowledge, and create scenes only of remembered events.

Giving myself imaginative freedom had cast me out on the open waters, and made me feel helpless all over again. This was not what contemplating a different fate for my father was supposed to be like.

I was supposed to give my father the years he never had, and then something would change, some unfulfillable desire would be satiated through my own creative abilities. He could be anything, anyone, and I could be the author of my own—our own—fate.

So I dove right into the writing, like a fiend chasing his final fix. Words rushed onto the page. I wanted to give him everything because I wanted to have everything. I became greedy. I wanted that hit of subjunctive morphine to course through my veins, and I knew it would never be enough. Every word, every moment, every detail put down required more.

I was not in control after all. Indeed, I did not want to be in control. What was this horrible feeling of having to *decide*? To make decision after decision about what would happen to my father. I wanted to give it all back and let destiny take the reins again, have its way with his life and mine.

This was when doubt and anxiety and sadness and anger entered my bloodstream to say, You may author your story, but there will be a cost. Out of fear, and an inability to deal with the immensity of his living, I retreated back into his death.

My partner and I passed the playground, usually filled with children and their high-pitched laughter but now empty and damp. From the corner of my eyes, I thought I saw a moving apparition and the empty swing rocking gently back and forth.

Finally, I responded to my partner in a voice barely perceptible to myself, "I just can't see another way." The turbulent sky above us began to rumble.

EARLIER THAT DAY, I HAD decided that my father would die in the story. Looking out the window at the steady sheet of falling rain, I saw, or thought I saw, the mundane logic of his death, a slow death common to older refugee men struggling in countries like the United States and Canada, relegated to hard, backbreaking lives. I told myself there was just no other way. No other ending felt right.

Of course, he would have to die at some point, as we inevitably do, but my realization meant that he would die *before his time, again*. It meant I'd have to kill him with my own typing fingers this time.

This decision was a relief—a weight lifted off my shoulders. I was able to lay down the large sphere of my father's expanding life.

Immediately after I had arrived at this decision, I got under the covers and took a nap. I had barely slept since I began writing about my father's fictional life, and I fell into a deep slumber. Then I started to dream.

In the corner of an empty room sits an old grey suitcase. I'm unable to unlatch its rusted lock with my fingers, and the more I try, the tighter the suitcase shuts, refusing to yield its contents to me. I struggle as if I know the dream is about to wash away.

My ex-brother-in-law suddenly appears and opens the suitcase with ease.

He hands the empty suitcase to me as half of it hangs open on the hinge. I stand there holding it by the handle—a no-longer-young man with rolled-up pant legs, my feet submerged in trickling water.

Despair fills my eyes, and a fist—maybe my own, maybe someone else's—punches through the side of the suitcase, revealing a hidden cache of black-and-white photographs.

The images are of my father as an old man with long, greying hair. They are of our family in Vietnam and in a placeless future. I see, for the first time, what my father looks like beyond the age of forty-six: an unassuming, undistinguished immigrant ravaged by time. The images are so clear and unmistakably real. These are photos I've never seen before. These are images of my unarticulated desire. I hastily gather them into a pile and hold on to them tight with both hands, pulling them toward me.

The room fills with water.

When I opened my eyes, I was crying. My tears flowed into the deluge outside. The drenched city felt unbearable. The sound of rainwater hitting my windows vibrated as aching ripples. It felt a little like drowning.

As MY PARTNER AND I followed the little curve in the path, I told him that the thought of my father's death at my own hands made the writing easier, that I had woken up from a delirious nap and written past an impasse in the story—the moment of our reunion in the United States—and words had fallen from a wound inside me to stain the page.

He didn't say anything in return, just kept in step with me, and I knew he loved me like I would never be loved again in this brief life.

As he reached for my hand, I told him how my therapist would carefully guide some of her patients toward a past trauma. How she'd ask them to pause seconds before the crucial moment—a car crash or a violent attack, for example—and pay attention to the sensations the body was experiencing. Then she would ask the patient to describe how they would react differently—to swerve to the other lane or kick the attacker in the shins and run. She gave them space to imagine another narrative, which would reactivate the nervous system, unfreeze the body, unstick what was stuck. She claimed that those who were able to get to this point experienced an easing of symptoms.

Listening to all this, my partner asked me if, in returning to my father's death to rewrite the story, I was also distancing myself from him. Was I working toward forgetting?

And that made me think of the summer I had spent wandering around cemeteries in the city during the pandemic. I'd made note of the ostentatious mausoleums with stone pillars and entranceways, and the humble, fading plaques set deep in the ground.

Graves are, of course, personal memorials, and cemeteries are places that make the past accessible. But what I saw that summer, over and over again, were relics of oblivion. Walking through the winding paths that led from one section of the deceased to another, I had thought how graves facilitate the letting go of memory for the living. Because the dead are buried there, because they are real and permanently beneath the granular earth, we can loosen our grip, just a bit, on our memories of them. We know where they are. The anxiety about their disappearance from our lives does not rise to the surface in the same way it does with a graveless death. At least they have a resting place, and we can visit them. So we make trips to the cemetery once or twice a year, and the rest of the time we simply live, wrapped up in little dramas, counting down the days.

Back on the winding path, I thought that if I became a bit more unstuck now, it was because I could capture my father's life and then box it in a wooden casket. I could bury it in a small plot of land, six feet underground. Writing it would make his death—and his life leading up to that death—neat and knowable. My words a marker of his place in this physical world, a story for me to hold and pass on to others. Somewhere I could visit and revisit.

Up ahead of us, the thwacking sound of a ball being hit echoed inside the fenced cage of the tennis court.

I thought that this imagined life for my father might displace his actual death in my mind, that his written death would become the new reality. I had erected a story as tombstone so I could forget. I would be the aging man with rolled-up pant legs tending to the grave, pulling up dandelions that had taken root, brushing off dry leaves that had landed on stone, lighting incense after incense with closed palms. I would walk across the lawn, exit the cemetery, and go back to a life that belonged to me.

I remembered my therapist saying that sometimes the exercise of return could be dangerous if not done with care. Which is why she always began with a comforting image or memory at the point of departure. After that, she would slowly walk her patient back toward the difficulty. This traffic between the safe present and the could-have-been future was a crucial buffer for the painful past.

My partner and I continued walking toward the southern end of the park. Heavy clouds filled and then merged in the sky, changing the quality of light below, dimming everything a deeper shade of dark. Moving our bodies under the building pressure, we were unaware that, underneath the ground, lush with spring grass and blooming trees, ran an ancient creek that still flowed toward one of the Great Lakes.

To create the park, city officials at the turn of the twentieth century gradually filled in the ravine and buried the creek. Since then, city dwellers converge on the park all year long, and in the summertime it comes alive with people cracking beers open, browning their skin, throwing footballs, unleashing dogs, and finding shelter—living on the surface while below something else is happening, a past life occurring in parallel. But during heavy rainfalls, the creek will sometimes reappear as brown flood water, turning the park into a haunted swamp demanding to be a stream again.

WHEN WE REACHED THE ARCHED gates, I realized that in killing my father, I'd get to know. That was it. I would get to know.

"I'd get to know," I said.

"What?"

I shifted my body closer to my partner, squeezing his fingers in my hand.

"I'd get to know *how* he dies."

I looked up at the sky and saw the clouds sagging with anticipation, pressing down on us. What I also understood in that moment was that my father's death, after more than three decades, had finally lifted.

I was propelled forward by magical thinking too. Bringing my father into the future—writing life back into his life—was my own necessary migration through the delay of death, the suspension of his dying, in order to hold him, and then slowly let him go.

We arrived at the southeastern corner, where rows of cherry trees lined the path. The earlier rain had battered the blossoms, scattering petals all over the wet ground. The once-full trees were now bare, branches not what they had been just a week before.

Above us, there was a sudden crack of lightning, followed by a bone-shattering roar. My father's death had given me this life that I had now. If he were alive, I wouldn't be me, and despite my share of disappointments and heartbreaks, I wouldn't want it any other way. I had come to prefer his death.

I've chosen my life, this life, over that of my father.

I'm a cruel son. My imagination has its limit.

The answer to my partner's question about why I needed to kill my father is that the pain I've carried has made me unable to give *myself* a happy ending.

"I just can't see another way," I tell him.

I need to survive in this world too.

Descending the five steps leading out to the sidewalk, we reached a large rectangular plaque set into the ground. It looked like a tombstone. On it was a map of Toronto and the outline of the crawling phantom creek that was hidden underground.

Stepping closer, I noticed that bordering the map were various words and symbols that indicated "water." Then I saw drops of rain splattering the oxidized metal. I moved my foot, and underneath where I was standing I saw four letters—*Nước*.

The intermittent drops became a downpour, and my partner and I turned west to head home. The city was a blur through the rain, which came down so fast it danced against everything it touched, creating a misty fog. In just a few seconds we were soaked, two figures floating through water, moving both forward and backward in time.

THE FORECAST CALLED FOR RAIN the day my mother drove my father to the hospital. But the rain never came, she told me when I called, as if that was an important thing to note.

She said, "Not good," when I asked how he was doing.

"Why didn't you tell me?" I accused her.

She told me that they hadn't wanted me to worry or be distracted from my studies. She said it was just a few headaches at first and then weakness, but men like him, they grow old and decline. Nothing seemed out of the ordinary. Nothing that couldn't have been fixed with nutritious soups and no smoking. My father kept on going to work on time, never missing a day. He'd stopped drinking too, and slept more. Things improved for a while and he regained his strength, committed to living a healthier life. My father—for a short time—thought he was just beginning again, that a new start was on the horizon. He even dared to imagine retiring in Vietnam, visiting his eldest daughter and her children in Minneapolis more often, meeting up with old friends in Florida for fishing trips, and seeing his youngest son's graduation exhibit in New York City.

This son, his favourite child, the one that he spoiled, had left the house because he wanted more than what they could give him. He wanted not to be tied down by the need to make money. But he didn't understand that wanting more was tempting good fortune to abandon you. He was thinking only of himself.

My father supported me anyway.

"Come back as soon as you can," my mother said before she hung up.

I went online to book the cheapest ticket back to California, which would take me through three cities over the course of thirty-two hours. It was a risk I had to take. It was all I could afford.

When I first left home for art school, my mother stopped talking to me. She was hurt; she felt as though she no longer knew me, like the things she worked hard to make happen had fallen apart.

A year later, she finally picked up the phone when I called home. She asked if I was well. She asked if I had eaten, as if nothing had changed. I said, "I can't be an accountant, Mom." She said, "I know. I just wanted you to have a better life than we did."

Standing in line with my backpack to speak to an agent about my cancelled second leg at the Newark airport, I wished I had become an accountant. Like a good son, I should have lived the life they desperately wanted for me.

WHAT HAPPENED NEXT, I WAS not there to witness. I gathered it only from the small bits of information fed to me whenever my mother and siblings felt like doing so, whenever a tiny crack appeared in their ironclad will to survive.

Overnight, he took a turn for the worse. He had difficulty breathing and vomited bile, because he hadn't eaten anything solid for days. When my second sister arrived at the hospital, he spoke Vietnamese to her, but none of the words made sense. He closed his eyes and gently shook his head from side to side.

The doctors noticed swelling. They stuck more needles and tubes into him. They came and went, making notes on their plastic clipboards.

My mother placed a wet cloth on his forehead.

The doctors said to prepare.

My mother whispered in his ear, "Wait."

His three children and his wife sat in the room, by his bedside.

Before the end, he did what all dying people miraculously do: regained a moment of lucidity.

There were tears.

He asked if we were all there.

"Yes," they lied.

Then, he was gone.

14

MOTHER NARRATOR

WHAT COMES AFTER KILLING ONE's father is guilt.

I didn't realize when I first began writing about him that I would end up with blood on my hands. Each word a stab wound. Each line a death sentence.

Cycling down a path swallowed by cruelty, my father encounters a son waiting to betray him with story.

I attempt a confession. I gather evidence against myself. But instead of going straight to my mother, I look for an old photo of us together.

On the back of the photo, my mother writes in quotation marks, "I'm very sad because Father is not beside me on my day of happiness." This is what little Vinh said on his seventh birthday in Ban Thad refugee camp. She refers to me as "cu," a common nickname for boys, which is also slang for penis or dick. The photo is an image of me seated next to my mother, so close it looks like I'm on her lap, the top of my head blending into her long, hanging hair. I'm holding an item of food to my mouth, smiling and looking content. On the table before us are dishes my mother has lovingly prepared—glistening vermicelli noodles mixed with crabmeat; pork spring rolls fried brown to perfection; translucent coconut jelly, set firm and cut into exact squares; and a bowl of steaming white rice.

I salivate for those familiar flavours. My stomach grumbles, craving the comfort of a mother's meagre extravagance. Such hunger makes me almost forget that the words my mother has put in my mouth seem a bit contrived, the grammar too complex. I suspect I would not—indeed could not—have used such diction to express my uncomplicated longing. The writing continues, "The children speak of you all the time." This sentence feeds my doubt. My mother has carefully chosen her words. She is telling a story to my father and creating the characters of his devoted children.

I found this photo the last time I visited Vietnam. My grandmother held on to it when my father left. It's one of the only things I can know for sure belonged to him. That I'm able to hold this photo in my hands now means that he received it and that he read a story about my life without him.

Sitting on the edge of the table, next to the food, is an inflatable blue bunny with cartoon eyes. Its innocence threatens to overtake the image. I have no memory of missing my father or asking after him. Looking at this photo, I don't think I'd ever been happier in my life.

I see that my mother has written me, written us. I'm not the first or only author of our lives. With these messages, my mother began our family memoir all those years ago, out of necessity, out of a desire to reach just one faithful reader.

WHEN I TELL MY MOTHER I've been writing a memoir, she asks what I remember. I say that what I don't remember I will imagine. She responds by saying she'll message me the dates and timeline of what happened. She says it's important to get the facts right, even if you have to make things up.

She calls and we talk about everything but my writing. She speaks about the orange sky and the smoke that has enveloped Calgary, blown in from wildfires up north. I ask her what she's made for supper. "Pan-fried basa filets and watercress soup, just something light and simple," she says. She asks if work is busy, and I respond with something generic about meetings and deadlines. She speaks about her mother, who died earlier in the year, and the different meanings of filial piety, especially the acts that others don't or can't see.

She asks what I've eaten, and I tell her some store-bought pizza. She wishes she could be there to cook for me, and I tell her soon, that I'm looking forward to her visit. Then there's a short pause. She asks what I'm doing. I think she's afraid of what I will get right about our story and of what I will get wrong.

I tell her that I'm writing. "About what?" she asks.

"Our escape from Vietnam," I say.

"You were very young, there were things you didn't know about," she says.

"Tell me," I say.

I promise that I'll send her the memoir when I have a full draft. She says, Okay. She tells me to drink more water. And to wear a hat in the sun.

I say, "Bye Mom."

And she says, "I love you," in English.

AND THAT'S HOW IT BEGINS. My mother writes a parallel memoir to my own.

She writes everything down by hand in a small blue note-book, and then she types it into an email to send to me. She says she will translate her words slowly into English so I can more easily comprehend what she has written. I tell her to wait and read it out loud to me when she visits, when we are face to face, but she wants to do it her way, to be in charge of how her story is received and when.

I check my email one day and see the first instalment, "Part 1: Our Journey to Flee from Vietnam," in my inbox. I click open the message and skim the long narrative she has sent, identifying precise dates and place names that have existed in my memory as redacted information. I sense that the story will take form in a way it has never taken form for me before. It's as if my mother is colouring in the outlines I've been tracing for decades, giving dimension to old shapes, making them fit together in my mind. She is propelling my narrative forward.

Yet I close the message without actually reading what she wrote. I realize that I can't. I'm afraid her version will bump up against mine, and knowing more will mean so many different revisions. So many new unknowns to accommodate. It will take me off track from the version that I need to tell for myself, one that I've become attached to because of the time I've spent developing it as a means of self-preservation. The possibility of having my story changed and challenged feels discomfiting. It feels a bit too real. And for the first time, I recognize how safe it was for me not to know certain things, to be protected by a child's fallible memory.

And there are also classes to teach, meals to be had with friends, and bathtubs to scrub. The stubborn present asserting itself yet again. I let mundane life become a buffer between what I know and what my mother knows. Now that she's ready to tell me everything, I'm not prepared to take it all in.

So my mother's story sits in my inbox, pushed down farther every day by new batches of emails—automatic bill notifications, work requests, and greetings from distant acquaintances. I let myself forget that her story is there waiting for me.

Then she messages to ask if I've read it and to remind me that her visit is upcoming. I don't respond. Instead, I spend the whole afternoon absorbed in running errands, preparing myself to read the first part of her memoir.

Late in the evening, under the bedcovers, I place my laptop on my chest and open her email. I begin reading with an open mind. The narrative she writes is chronological and straightforward. It begins on the night before we left Vietnam and ends with our safe arrival in Cambodia, before we got on a boat for Thailand. The story contains many facts and is written in a direct, confessional tone.

My mother writes clearly, and her sentences are well composed. The first few lines, though, do not prepare me for the charge of the writing. There's a sharp emotional clarity in sentences like, "Daddy lay beside me—even we knew this night was the last night we stayed together, but we couldn't talk anything. The feeling uneasy, fearful, scared, worried all like dancing in our minds."

To see unease, fear, and worry join hands in the dark, creating distance between these two people who are my parents, makes my heart, beneath the heat of the laptop, contract. I could stay in this reclined position forever. I wish I could have occupied that silence with them.

What my mother gives me in her words is texture—texture to experiences that I now don't have to make up in my mind. What I've always had was the fact of my parents as people. To me, they are individuals who went through difficult things, things that many other people like them also went through. What I have never had is access to how they did this, what they felt, what living looked like for them.

My mother's memoir does more than give dimension to dull shapes. It makes their story bloom in my mind, taking root in empty plots, decorating my imagination with bougainvillea real enough to bring my nose toward and inhale. And as I read on, I take no notice of dates and place names, when and where things happened, how time unfolded. Knowing the precise facticity of the situation does not propel me much further than where I've dwelled for so long.

The story's situation does not matter anymore. What I need are the details and figurative language my mother brings to our lives, her curation of what is meaningful to tell and what is significant to know, her voice conveying more than what is actually written.

Her narrative delivers the thing I've been chasing—the *art* of our lives.

She writes that we took a bus from Tây Ninh, Vietnam, and crossed the border over into Cambodia. After a long, tiring journey, everyone was hungry. She mentions that we wandered through the market looking for food—a forty-year-old woman holding her children close in a strange new place—and I hear the hard clicks of the Khmer tongue floating through the stalls, and smell the pungent fish paste mixed with the acrid sewer. I see the clouds begin to spit drops on the ground, forming little dark clumps. She writes that we ate Phnom Penh rice noodles, a local specialty, and I can taste the pork bone broth, the fried garlic, the buttery liver. In her description she says it was "delicious, like nothing that can be imagined." I see five figures hunching over steaming bowls, slurping broth into eager mouths, smiling with our eyes, stomachs satiated—our first meal as refugees.

My mother's memoir writing gives new structure to her days. She wakes up in the morning, eats her usual breakfast of oats and bananas, and then sits down to write. She is disciplined, spending hours and hours filling lines on the page, her trusted guide an old and torn Vietnamese-English dictionary. She flips the thin, crisp pages, looking for the exact words as her glasses slip from the bridge of her nose.

She tells me that doing this work is testing her memory. She is going to places unvisited for many decades.

She sends me "Part 2: A Long Way To No Where," which begins: "It's not easy to think of the past that I didn't want to remember. A unhappy past that I had buried more than thirty years ago."

I consider deleting this email, reading no further. There is no point. I consider telling her to stop, to keep it all buried.

But then I wonder what remembering is doing for her. Is she now seeing these stories outside herself for the first time? Can she let them go? Or ponder their significance? That she has to plot out events, and then put words to how she feels, means she must examine her hitherto unexamined life.

My mother hasn't had the luxury of reflection. Reflection is for women without four children to raise; reflection is for women with husbands and free time; reflection is for women who buy multiple dresses and leave them hanging in the closet, tags still on.

I call and ask how she's doing and try to gauge any change in the quality of her voice. Has she been crying? Has she slept? Are her memories hurting her?

"Do you want to stop writing, Mom?"

"No. I like it. It gives me something to do."

"Are you okay?"

"Everything's okay. Everything I write, it's for you."

"For me?"

My mother digs through layers of sedimented experience to produce material for me to use in my memoir. This practical element of remembering—to help and support her child—is what makes it possible. She needs a reason to bring up the past again in a way that is not frivolous but utterly necessary. An action with an outcome—a story, a book to hold in her hands.

The value of my mother's story is tethered to the memoir I'm writing. She gives and she gives, like she always has, and she lets me do whatever I want with the heft of her memories. I refashion them into my own and put words in her mouth, making what I feel into what she feels. I acquire more evidence for my guilt. I may be the author of this story, but I'm also a little boy hanging on to her leg, peeking out at the strange world from behind the refuge of my mother.

=

I read my son's story. I tell him it's very good. I am proud of him.

In Vietnam, I take my children to fortune teller.

The fortune teller say we survive. But not my husband. He see only five people walk through the airport door. Not six. Not my husband.

I didn't want to believe it.

But it is all true.

It is fate.

He say the young one, he can do anything other people do.

And it came true.

I have no expectation from him. I only want him to be good person. Happy and good person.

And he make me so proud.

WHEN I READ THE STORY, I get very emotional, because it is good story about our family. But I don't have the English language to understand everything completely, although I went to school in Canada and get my GED diploma. Like high school diploma. Not many people same like me have that. My sisters who came to Canada before I came didn't get it.

But now I am also too old. The words they no longer inside my head. They disappear. Fly away.

I think I understand only some of the meaning. But I read every word. I try to.

About why we leave Vietnam. Living in refugee camp. Coming to Canada. The difficulty of life. Losing his father.

HIS WRITING IS VERY GOOD, but he didn't know a lot of things. Many information he got wrong. For example, we come to Canada in 1990 not 1991. He forget. Our border crossing was mostly going on land. We didn't go on a boat from Vietnam but Cambodia. And also another example I was feeling fear when he tell me he is gay. My heart pounding. Many fears. I'm not so strong as he think. And his father, he sends many documents and photos to Canada before he left. I threw everything in the garbage.

THERE ARE MANY THINGS MY son doesn't know.

HIS STORY IS NOT COMPLETE. His story is only a small understanding.

I THINK IT'S NOT GOOD to not get the details right. A story should move from beginning to ending. Facts have to be true, because we don't want people to believe something that did not happen. Why?

===

I THINK HIS STORY IS not organized. Why there are too many stories together, from here and here and here. He moving around too much. No before and after. It's not straightforward. I like straightforward stories.

ALSO I DON'T THINK WHAT he wrote is very believable. Like his father being alive. Is too far from reality. Too idealistic.

WHY SHOULD HE WRITE THAT story?

MAYBE HE NEED TO IMAGINE so he can have no more questions in his heart. Like the heavy lifted from him.

BUT WHY HE WRITE A book for everyone to read?
    Isn't that more heavy?
    I think the story is private.
    It should be for family only.
    Sometimes I don't understand.

WHEN I SEE HE IS writing about me, I think who is this woman. Some details correct, but it's like he writing about another woman similar to me but is not me.

Why did he make me say those things like that? Why did he make up my words in the story? I didn't write that to him. I don't remember the events he wrote. Did I say that I thought. Oh when did it happen?

I don't think he is writing about me or his father.

He writing about the things inside his head only.

But I don't say this to him.

WHEN I VISIT HIM IN Toronto I say good job my boy.

He smiled and he hugged me.

He ask me if reading make me sad.

I say no, nothing make me sad now.

Nothing.

BUT I THINK THAT HE is looking back too much.

I tell him that in life you have to only look forward. Look forward only, okay.

Look at the people who look back. They stuck in the past. They regrets. They cannot live. Go crazy.

You write, but don't look back all the time I tell him.

It's very dangerous.

I have experience. I can warn him to avoid the things that are not good.

=

ONE DAY I SAY TO him he should drink more water or he will get sick.

>The sun is too hot. There will be dehydration.
>
>Wear a hat.
>
>He say mom why you say again and again.
>
>I say I only remind you.
>
>He say okay I'm not a baby.
>
>I say you always my baby. I know what is good for you.
>
>I am you mother.
>
>After that he didn't say anything all day.

THEN I TAKE A WALK by myself. I walk and walk almost to Chinatown.

>Toronto is full of people. Always like festival.
>
>My son he have a good life here.
>
>Sometime he don't know that.
>
>So much to be grateful about.
>
>He shouldn't be unhappy.
>
>He can lose everything.

I AM WORRIED IF PEOPLE read his book and they don't understand his story.

>What will happen to him?
>
>He is exposed to the whole world.
>
>What if he will lose everything?

＝

WHAT IF HE LOSE HIMSELF?
Anything can happen.
I know.

SO WHEN I LEAVING TORONTO to go back to Calgary I say pro-
tect yourself.
He say I know, I know.
I mean when you write you should make sure it's the right
story you want to tell.
Don't be influenced from other people.
They don't know you.
You don't have to tell any story you don't want to.
Tell our story simply.
Even though our story is not so simple.
But I don't say this out loud to him.
I say bye bye I love you and then I go on the airplane.

15

FLIGHTS

MY MOTHER TELLS ME SHE wants to visit me in Toronto.

At the airport, she comes through the sliding doors wheeling a carry-on suitcase with a Teflon pan and a giant roll of Costco plastic wrap inside. Later, when she opens the suitcase and gives me the pan and plastic wrap, I will chuckle and, half admonishing her, say that I have no use for such things. Later still, frying chicken in the pan, using a recipe she taught me, I'll remember her small figure against the sharp shine of the metal doors, searching for a familiar face just beyond the threshold, crowded out by pale figures that tower over her. I'll use the wrap to keep the leftover chicken fresh. The roll, like my naive trust in her enduring presence, will last forever.

In the taxi, she gently cups her hand to my face and asks, "Are you happy?" without actually saying it. I turn and reply, "Are you lonely?" with my reticent eyes.

What sits in between us is the space of a man.

The things we want to say to each other get lost in this open space. If they arrive, the phantom words are tattered, missing a diacritic or a vowel, as if dragged through a storm. This space is the shared memory that holds us together: her memories are more vivid and plentiful, even if age has scrambled their order or dulled the edges, while my memories are wanting, even if they have finally become real through the fiction of writing. This space is oblivion, or the things we must forget to stay anchored to this world. This space is what keeps us vigilant, never hoping for too much. This space in the shape of a man is death, which slammed into a boat and delivered us to the quiet lives we lead now.

I roll down the window to let in some air, and watch brick buildings, framed by verdant trees on a residential street, pass by. The families that live in them will not know how war can creep up the driveway at night, force itself through the locked door, and snatch husbands away with zip ties, leaving a man-sized wound on the back of their future.

She rolls her window down too. The breeze ruffles her hair, and the sunlight makes her squint. This little gesture, unseen by me, is what my mother has learned to do to protect herself over the years, what she's mastered into an art of living.

She picks up the conversation to tell me, without using words, that being in a couple is complicated. That's why she has chosen to remain alone, not for lack of suitors—a devoted admirer in the refugee camp, a reunited childhood crush, a married man willing to part with his wife, among others. There have been opportunities to start over again with someone, but it has just been too complicated, she sighs silently.

I don't ask what she means. I will understand only later what complication feels like. But it's not the fights and compromises with my partner that teach me the lesson. It's the knot in my stomach whenever he packs for a trip, the nightmare sleep while he's away, the daily anticipation of loss. The fear that he will not return to me is a bloated body always surfacing in the open waters of my mind.

My mother has realized that being alone is a safe certainty. Because the possibility of loving someone and then losing them—again—is too much to repeat in one lifetime. This is not trauma but the prudence of experience.

I wish that she had someone to spend her final years with. But when my hair has greyed, and lines sprawl over my face, I'll accept that this wish was just my own regret for not having been there, for living my own life instead of trying to reconstruct a past one with her.

Then, she'll come to me in a dream and say, "We've already died once, what's the point of living for others?"

The taxi driver finds it odd that we sit in silence. He considers asking if we want the radio turned on, but decides against it when he looks into the rear-view mirror and sees an arm stretched across his field of vision, moving toward a face to reposition a stray hair.

He sees, for the first time, our resemblance.

The taxi makes its way through the dense urban landscape, the sidewalks dappled with shadows, people and their dogs, bicycles weaving between cars.

Later, I ask her to make an elaborate meal—of turmeric crepes and scallion meatballs, lotus salad and crab soup—for my friends. My mother finds a raptured audience of gay men, immigrants themselves, all squeezed into my tiny condo, longing for small acts of family. She understands maybe half of the conversation in English and laughs freely.

She makes herself at home.

Before she leaves, my mother asks me about my trip to Vietnam and Thailand. Both places she's become unfamiliar with over the years.

She says, "Tell me—tell me, what did you see, what did you find, what did you feel?"

Are you still the same person?

16

FALLING IN REVERSE

Inside Narita Airport's Terminal 1, I spot a group of Vietnamese men dressed in full army fatigues. They are heading to the homeland, looking for the same gate as me. I drag my carry-on behind them, keeping enough distance so I can listen in on their conversation but still remain unseen, separated from their orbit.

I listen as they discuss what the weather will feel like when we land in Saigon, and where to smoke a cigarette now. Their Southern Vietnamese accent is thick and unbridled, their skin dark and weathered. Figures gaunt. They look like they've just stepped out of a decades-old battlefield. They look like they are still fighting a war. I wonder what part of the diaspora they've arrived from and what pulls them back here. I want to close the gap between us, to share a cigarette with them and ask if they've been away for as long as I have. Instead, I just follow them, the wheels of my suitcase rattling against the tiled floor.

When we reach Gate 25, I see more Vietnamese people in one place than I have seen for a long time. They are spread out across the waiting area, sleeping off long connecting flights, eating food they've packed, or fiddling on electronic devices. I begin to feel more at ease, as if my reintroduction to the foreign place called Vietnam has already begun here in this airport. A small dose of what's to come, so I'm not overwhelmed just yet.

Some people have already started lining up to board the plane. The line quickly builds and winds along the walkway. Surveying the queue, I think I can spot us in any crowd. There's something distinctive about our look, something close to weariness, or a stubborn will to push forward, that reveals itself beneath any outfit, haircut, or layer of makeup.

The men in fatigues join the line, and I do the same. As announcements are made over the intercom, an indistinct chatter starts to build around us. Vietnamese words float through the air, mixing with Japanese and an anxious energy. I open the passport in my hand, checking to see if the photo page is still there—scanning, once more, the information written on it to make sure I am really who I claim to be.

Surname/Nom
 NGUYEN
Given Names/Prénoms
 VINH
Nationality/Nationalité
 CANADIAN/CANADIENNE
Sex
 M
Place of Birth/Lieu de naissance
 HO CHI MINH CITY VNM

For the first time, I think about the difference between my nationality and my place of birth. I ponder the vast distance, realizing how long it takes to go from one place to the other. The logistics of flight, the physical toll it takes on the sojourner— how the body is bent out of shape and confused in movement; how it sleeps when it should be awake and stays up when it should be sleeping. The mind, too, has to relocate, to wind and rewind time, see everything anew.

I'm comforted knowing that my Canadian identity will allow me to pass through the gate, the air, the border, and the customs kiosk. I inch forward and forward until I'm standing at the front being wished a good flight, moving along the connecting bridge, stepping onto the plane, and buckling myself in. As the captain signals the flight attendants to prepare for takeoff, I'm struck with the sudden fear that a passport will allow me to sink slowly into a past that I might not be able to come back from.

• • •

SEVEN HOURS LATER, JUST PAST midnight, I land in Tân Sơn Nhất Airport. The line to enter the country moves quickly, and I become just another visa number to pass through, a small source of tourism revenue; the officer barely even looks up to see who I am before he flicks the back of his hand.

When I get into a taxi and peer out the window as it drives off, Ho Chi Minh City is all light and shadow, not yet real. The driver asks what I plan to see while I'm visiting and, like all genuine Vietnamese people, proceeds to tell me what to do, what is good for me: go to Phú Quốc, where the sand is soft; enjoy the wild parties on Bùi Viện Street, where all the foreigners hang out; don't visit Hanoi in the winter, when the cold bites; and, most importantly, reconnect with your homeland while there is still time. His forthrightness is so familiar, so calming, that I almost ask him to keep driving so we can escape the coming dawn together.

As he pulls up outside my hotel, I situate myself momentarily in space. I've been on this street before, I recognize even in the dark. And, just like that, a fifteen-year absence from the city vanishes.

I spend the next twenty-two hours asleep. I don't dream and I don't wake up until the sun has set on another day, until my stomach grumbles.

Emerging from the cocoon of my curtained hotel room onto the bustling street, the moist heat and the roar of motorbikes hit me like a gut punch, stinging me awake from deep inside. I see neon electrifying buildings and families holding hands. Foreigners drink "333" beers on terraces. A light breeze blows in from the Saigon River and I think how much I have aged.

I turn down a narrow alley and remember the last time I was here, how I carried only a small backpack and owned one pair of leather sandals, traversing the city like a young man free for the first time from his identity—Vietnamese or Canadian, Asian or Western, local or foreigner. I did the backpackers' circuit, staying in hostels and takings buses all over the country.

And then I remember two years before that, when I returned to Vietnam for the first time, with my mother, sister, and then brother-in-law. How I thought I was free from being my mother's son. How I swatted her hand away when she tried to hold on to me in a large crowd. How I dismissed her suspicion of everyone, seeing it not as her embodied experience but as her irrationality. I made her cry by refusing to sit next to her on a four-hour train ride.

I was in my early twenties both times I was here previously, and both times, I was a different person. I am someone else now.

The city too was another city: younger, fewer tall buildings, closer to the war. I wonder who I will be and what the city will have become the next time I return.

I don't know Ho Chi Minh City at all, is what I think to myself as I continue walking into a maze of alleyways. Drop me in London or Paris and I will know which tube or metro to take to get to my destination; I will point out the famous sites and places to eat, describe neighbourhoods in close detail—will have a mental map of the city in my mind. But Saigon, Ho Chi Minh City, the place of my birth, remains elusive. A place of being lost, a place where I am lost to myself.

I come here because this is the place I know to go for answers. I can't admit to myself that it's a place of questions and endless tempting alleys that lead to dead ends.

I think about how we count years, about the repetition of time, and I realize I'm now the same age as my mother was when she left this city for good. I can't fathom what it would be like to become an new person at forty, to risk it all and start again. I want my forty-year-old mother to know she will be okay. I want to let her hook her slender arm into mine and guide her to a safer place, where cruel life can't find her. I want to tell her that I am here.

At forty, my father had six more years to live. Six years is the age I lost him. At forty, my father had been free from imprisonment for just over a year and had become a new father for the fourth and final time. At forty, my father was beginning a short-lived new life. I had only five years with him, few enough to be counted on one small hand.

One. Một.
Two. Hai.
Three. Ba.
Four. Bốn.
Five. Năm.

I enter a restaurant that serves fried spring rolls filled with crabmeat. The waitress greets me first with casual familiarity and then, when she realizes something is not quite right, that I am not from around here, with polite apprehension. I order in Vietnamese, but when the food arrives, I struggle to ask for a napkin. I say the words for *paper* and *mouth*, and she scrunches her face in confusion. The fragrance of hot oil and sweet fish fills the air. As the mounted wall fan oscillates left and right, I am sitting next to myself watching myself watch another person trying to figure me out.

WHEN MY PARTNER ARRIVES THE next day, we go to Nguyễn Huệ walking street together. We start at one end by the river and move toward the other end, a statue of Hồ Chí Minh standing prominently in the middle of the boulevard, sectioned off by a narrow square moat where lotus flowers grow. In between, young men sing into microphones connected to amplifiers, skateboarders do kick-flips, teenagers practise K-pop dance routines, venders sell inflated toy animals and grilled rice paper "pizzas," young lovers entangle themselves on parked motorbikes, and families stroll—an entire new generation moving forward together.

These young people do not know war.

It's what makes them so beautiful in my eyes.

When we reach the statue, I tell my partner to pose under

Uncle Ho while I snap a photograph on my phone. In this photo, Uncle stands erect and dignified on a pedestal, with his right arm raised toward the sky and Vietnam's bright Communist future. Behind him stands the City Hall, lit up like the world's fair, a relic of the country's French colonial past. My partner, or anyone wanting a picture with Uncle, seems small and insignificant in this frame.

The statue's placement conveys historical progress, Vietnam's hard-won independence from foreign domination, but zoom out and the raised arm is pointing to the Chanel storefront underneath a luxury five-star hotel—the Rex. This is the actual future, the one that came true in the place that was once the vanguard of revolutionary imagination.

And why shouldn't Uncle's children have black leather bags with gold double-C clasps or sleep on thousand-thread-count Egyptian cotton sheets? It's a bile-churning shame that so many had to die in a too-long war for the country to decide that this is what it wants—participation in the global capitalist market as a bit player. This was what we went to war for and then won the right to?

So many of us, including my family, paid dearly for this.

I taste a metallic, slightly sour flavour in my mouth.

There is no better visual frame for Vietnam's twenty-first-century freedom than this one, I think bitterly—or is it *bereftly*?—to myself.

· · ·

THE NEXT WEEK WE FLY to Hanoi, the city of my parents' birth, the one of their first exile. This is where my ancestors came from. My partner and I circumnavigate the perimeter of Hồ Hoàn Kiếm, the lake where the legendary King Lê Lợi returned the magical sword given to him to defeat Chinese colonists and liberate Vietnam, not for the first or last time. Imagine the King placing the blade between the teeth of the Golden Turtle god in the lake. Imagine coming back home a hero. Imagine having the ability to restore nature's order and make everything have a place in the world.

I conjure my parents holding hands as they follow the steps of countless others who have walked the edges of this ancient lake, as my partner and I retrace them now. But my father never returned to Hanoi after evacuating the city. If he's ever walked around the lake, it was probably alone.

I have nothing to offer the Golden Turtle who has majestically floated around for centuries with a sword fastened on his back, so I drop a Canadian loonie, a dollar coin, into the jade-green water instead. I wonder if I should make a wish, if this lake grants miracles for prodigal sons who've achieved nothing heroic.

The next morning at the hotel's breakfast buffet, my partner and I sit next to a large American family on their last morning in the city. The children devour the eggs and bacon stacked on their plates, and the parents gush about everything Vietnamese. A waiter arrives with a tropical drink for the father. The usual for a regular, how all wait staff make tips by providing that extra personal touch. The father is delighted. He tells the waiter that he's going to miss seeing him in the mornings, that everyone here has made their stay so comfortable and meaningful. They are leaving the city feeling like they're a part of the family—"We will always remember you, brother." The father's drawing of kinship is expressed so sincerely I almost want to get up and give him a pat on the shoulders. I smile instead, and take a bite of my burnt toast.

Then I become curious how this white American has found his Vietnamese family so easily. I wonder if he's a returning GI, experiencing a different tour of the war-worn country. I wonder if he could give me some pointers and tell me where to find my family too.

In the afternoon, my partner and I explore the Old Quarter, where each street still bears the name of the wares it sells—like silver, paper, and bamboo. We wander aimlessly from shop to shop. Then, when we enter an artisan souvenir store with colourful puppets, figurines, and jewellery, the owner sidles up to me and, in Vietnamese, says, "Can I ask you a slightly odd question? I ask because *I am like you*. Are you," leaning closer to me, "*gay?*" He says the word *gay* in English. I nod.

"Are you from Saigon?" he then asks. I tell him that I live abroad. He exclaims that that's even better! Society here, he shares, is still not so accepting. They don't understand us just yet. "Take me, for example," he continues, "my family doesn't talk to me. I'm abandoned."

I look around and see that this shop is his house, and these trinkets are the new family he's amassed. He's never left his homeland, yet he too is searching.

He, this Vietnamese orphan, comes all the way to the entrance to wave us goodbye. This brief interaction reminds me that there are many ways for families big and small, national and nuclear, to break: war, death, politics, money, honour, migration, desire. The list goes on and on. It takes just one little thing, and it takes everything. It takes nothing too.

Hanoi remains the home of others.

I FLY BACK TO Ho Chi Minh City by myself because my partner's tourist visa won't let him stay any longer. His Turkish nationality makes it harder for him to remain in the place I was born. My Canadian passport buys me a few more days here. I must finish this prolonged return, this final act of falling, alone.

I spend my days wandering the city with no particular place to go and no purpose in mind. I walk in and then out, and then out and then in the hotel's double doors. I go up and then down the same streets. When it gets too hot in the afternoons, I take shelter in a café. I watch people move about their day as Christmas songs play in the unbearable December heat. I eat to get full. I sleep early at night.

One day, I visit my aunt's house, my father's youngest sister. I ask her if there's anything left that belongs to him, if my grandmother kept any of his things—a shirt, a notebook, a vase, some letters. Anything. She tells me that if there's anything, it might be in the storage cubby on the second floor. We head up together and pull out two cardboard boxes full of dust, the corners of which have been chewed through by rats. What we find inside are a few albums with mould growing on them, some old file folders with useless papers inside, and a rotted blanket. "Nothing," she says, "there is nothing."

BACK AT MY HOTEL THAT night, I switch on the TV for the first time. Flipping through the channels aimlessly in the dark, I chance upon a movie from the late 1950s—grainy images in Technicolor, framed by a small square. It takes a few minutes for me to understand that the movie is an adaptation of Homer's *The Odyssey* dubbed into Vietnamese.

I watch as Odysseus and his men drive a spike into the eye of the Cyclops. And then there's a scene of him standing at the prow of a ship in the open waters, navigating his way homeward, fated by the gods to end up on a detour, again and again, lost to his family, exiled from his life indefinitely.

I realize that I wasn't expecting to find anything. Whatever answers I could find in Vietnam would only open up more questions. This I had known in the edges of my mind but could not allow myself to admit. To really understand this, I had to travel thousands of miles to sit on a hotel bed alone in the dark.

Time does not wait for those returning.

My father is, and will always be, a character I come back to during difficult moments to write and rewrite. There is no finding him. There is just inventing him anew.

All the things that have troubled me—that my father is dead, that he died in unknown circumstances, that he might not actually be dead, that his afterlife lingers, that I have to live some of this life for him—all that, all this, will continue to trouble me until my time is up.

I think back to years ago, when I was chasing certainty without knowing what that looked like. I wanted anything that made me feel less unmoored. I wanted an anchor to hang on to. My father whole and complete.

But after all these years, my father will only flicker into the light and then retreat back into shadows. He will appear as a flash and then slip through the door. I will hold his arm, real and hefty, one moment, and the next he will be a curl of rising smoke.

The truth, the real truth, is no person can give me certainty. Not my father.

What is a father?

A father is one who leaves.

ODYSSEUS, THE FIRST REFUGEE RECORDED in story, leaves behind a wife and son as he wanders the stormy Ionian Sea seeking hospitality, and longing to return to his native land. After a hard-fought war and twenty years drifting from one island to another, nothing is more important to him than this homecoming, to reunite with his family and set foot again on the soil of his ancestors.

But while he is away, life stands still for his wife, Penelope, who refuses the advances of lecherous suitors, and his son, Telemachus, who searches for his missing father, learning about him only through the stories others tell.

The father's absence launches the son out on dangerous waters to look for answers. Before he embarks on his journey, the goddess Athena, in human disguise, reassures the son that his father is indeed still alive and will soon reappear. The ending, she foretells, like in all good mythology, is already determined, fated by a divine power.

Then she, with all her omnipotence, asks Telemachus a surprising and shattering question: Are you, in fact, Odysseus's child? The question reframes the quest. Undoes the lashing of the ship's planks, letting water pass through. What makes you his? And what makes him yours? After twenty years without him—your entire life really—what claims do you have on this father?

Who *are* you?

This interrogation elicits a poignant response from Telemachus, who has had his identity called into question, who must reckon with why he continues to chase a ghost to find himself: *My mother says indeed I am his. I for my part do not know. Nobody really knows his own father.*

Telemachus's answer penetrates the literal surface of Athena's question, diving down toward the vast chaos of the cosmic human heart. In the end, no one has real knowledge of their father, he explains.

For the father is his own person, a pyre of mystery even to himself, a shooting star leaving behind a dusty trail in the infinite darkness. A father escapes his son's embrace. He slips away from his daughter's hooked fingers. A father is a negative figure, undeveloped in the family photograph.

Nobody knows their own father, and nobody ever will.

THE ONLY OBJECT BELONGING TO my father that still survives is his driving permit.

Here it is. Let me show it to you.

Number: 039070

It's printed on thick pink paper that has decayed through the decades. The first fold is ripped and barely hangs on to the rest of the permit. A few more openings and closings, I think, will tear this first fold from the other panels. On the front, everything is written thrice, in Vietnamese, French, and English: the languages of early-1970s Vietnam, the languages of warfare. This document contains his date of birth, address, and signature. It says what vehicles he is allowed to operate. It tells me he was able to use a jeep or a motorbike to travel from here to there, there to here. The permit makes me think—wish—that he could've driven away, far from a world that constrained men like him—a small backpack on his shoulders, a helmet for protection—through the mountains and across the Cambodian border, along the jungles and paved roads of Thailand, the hills and valleys of Burma, the plains and rivers of Bangladesh, to arrive perhaps at the foot of the Himalayas. From there it is up to him to go wherever it pleases him, young, free, and alone.

I CARRY THIS PERMIT WITH me everywhere.

HOLD IT TIGHT. DON'T LET it slip from your fingers.

THE MIGRANT RAIN, I HAVE come to realize, are tears.

THE MIGRANT RAIN FALLS.

AFTER MANY WEEKS IN VIETNAM, which feels both too long and not long enough, I leave the country.

17

CHONBURI

After a week apart, my partner and I meet up in Bangkok to seek out Phanat Nikhom. It no longer exists, of course, but after several Google deep dives—wading through government files, reports, and dissertations looking for a good map—I finally stumble upon a former refugee who has also sought out the camp's location, retraced his old life. Fortunately for me, he has documented it all on his seldom-viewed YouTube channel. This amateur refugee historian, this fellow vigil keeper. I only know where to go because he has already made the trip.

Since there is no address, I watch his videos and take screenshots of all the landmarks that will lead me back there. The most precise clue for locating the camp is a road sign for a military station: 2nd Battalion, 111th Infantry Regiment. The former camp site, supposedly, sits across from this newly built barracks.

"This is where I want to go," I message the Thai driver we've hired, after I send him the image of the road sign. My phone screen tells me he is typing for a long time, but he responds twenty minutes later with a simple "Ok."

The driver picks us up early in the morning, and we inch our way outside the city's urban sprawl. When the landscape begins to change, fewer buildings and more empty fields, I ask him again if he can find the place I'm looking for.

"Yes." He smiles into the rear-view mirror.

His reassurance does not ease my anxiety, because deep down I already know that the camp cannot be found. What I'm looking for is the remains of a transitory place. What I'm looking for is lost time. Some other version of myself left behind.

And yet I must go. Take this drive down the dusty road anyway.

As he continues driving, my partner and I discuss what we will have for dinner when we return to the city, when all this is finally behind me. We decide on a Michelin-recommended place with rave reviews and modern aesthetics. The incongruence of it all—my incredible ability to move back and forth—will only register in my consciousness much later. Like my story, I am filled with unbridgeable contradictions.

• • •

THE DRIVER DROPS US OFF at the main entrance of the camp. "Bye, bye." He jokes that he'll see us back in Bangkok, and we all laugh. But a part of my helpless mind begs him not to abandon us at this site, not to make me a refugee once more, which seems almost possible at this moment.

The carcass of a long-dead animal lies in front of the entrance, which has a sign against digging, lest the electrical wires underground be hit and everything goes up in flames.

We slowly follow the paved road into an area lined with lush trees. Up ahead, there's a concrete structure that looks like a house and hung lines with clothes drying on them. People live here, it is clear, and I wonder why I ever believed the site would be abandoned, preserved for someone like me to return to. Why do I expect nothing to change, except myself?

I take out my phone and begin snapping photos. Perhaps when I see these images later, I will see this place for what it really is—a plot of land covered in soil, supporting verdant vegetation and human lives. A place wholly unspectacular and insignificant.

I will, later, send these images to my siblings, who will respond with more questions for me: Is the big central canteen still there? What happened to the ditches? Where are the boundaries? How did you find this place? Why were you there? I will tell them that I've needed to return for some time. What's in the images is all that's left. This place belongs to others now.

People have built new lives here. Farther down the road, my partner and I see a collection of simple buildings put together from wood, cement, and corrugated tin. In front of one building, a shirtless man is sprawled out on a mat, fanning himself to keep the flies away. Banana and jackfruit trees litter the path toward a small school. As we pass, three children standing at the entrance follow us with their eyes, wondering who we are, these two strangers who've invaded their afternoon.

While the camp is no longer here and time has changed so much, life is still the same. Houses still have thatched roofs, men still walk around barefoot, and I'm still a lonely child looking for my father.

As we turn down a red dirt path, a swarm of mosquitoes begins eating our exposed flesh, creating instant welts on our skin. We frantically wave them away and scratch our limbs as we walk, looking like two out-of-place fools.

When we get deeper onto the path, a dog appears in a yard and begins aggressively barking at us. And then another and another in other yards, all keeping guard. The neighbourhood reverberates with their loud warnings. A woman appears briefly at a doorway to survey the commotion.

We turn around and, with as much calm as we can muster, begin to retrace our steps back toward the entrance. The first aggressor, the dog who spotted us, follows behind on the path, herding us out with its bared teeth, making sure we get nowhere close to what it's supposed to protect. Fear, and the intense midday sun, drenches us in sweat.

If I didn't already know I don't belong here, these dogs have made sure that this poor, unremarkable neighbourhood will not be disturbed by a ghost coming back to dig up a long-buried past.

These dogs know. They perceive the danger of falling in reverse. Leave it alone, they say, and go back to the life you already have.

Leave.

When we reach the entrance, there has been no nostalgia, no longing, no reflection. My partner and I might have just spent an afternoon wandering through any random rural hamlet in Thailand. This might not even be the place where Phanat Nikhom used to be. Standing here, I don't feel any sense of affinity or recognition. I don't feel anything special, anything that I expected or wanted to feel.

Then I hear a faint rustling in one of the trees. I look up and see a little boy with his legs wrapped around a thick branch, his stomach resting on its length. He makes eye contact with me and smiles a wily smile. He waves one hand, and I wave back. And just as my partner opens the waiting car's door, the boy throws something at us. I can't make out what it is—a rock, a fruit, a nugget of wisdom—as I step inside the safety of the vehicle that will bring me back to the life I lead.

Inside, I tell the driver we're ready to leave. I'm comforted by the contained interior of the car, its tinted windows, which hide me from the world outside. I sink back into the present. We take the 120-kilometre route back to Bangkok, and I think about the many refugees, including my family, who have sat on an old bus, travelling this exact route toward a waiting plane and a life they could not yet imagine. Our car drives through a halo of dust kicked up by the truck in front.

●　●　●

THAT NIGHT, I DON'T SLEEP. Or I sleep, but I don't sleep well. I jolt awake in a panic of sweat, and the groaning AC sends shivers down my body. I don't know if I dreamt the day or if it really happened. I'm not sure where I am or where I've been. The only thing that might be real in this moment is the solid feeling lodged in my chest. I can't tell what it is, but only what it's like: a tense fist; gunpowder packed tight inside a bullet; the undercurrent of a wave; sitting astride a moving elephant; a train coming to a sudden halt; an apple falling to the ground with a thump; the weight of a hand on top of another hand.

An apparition passing through a door.

Everything, I think, is known imperfectly. The answers I'm seeking cannot be accessed through the fact of things, but only by the residual sensations that linger in the body, the blurry images that fortify memory, and the searing truths that set feeling afire.

In the freezing hotel room, I accept that I've reached the edge of my narrative. It is the literal, physical end. There is nowhere else for me to go from here.

What has been found? I ask.

ONLY MYSELF—

· · ·

A PERSON WHO IS STILL alive.

A person who must return—not to the past but to a waiting mother in Calgary.

A person who is defined, at the core, by uncertainty.

Without reliable truth.

Free from any one ending.

Wedded to none.

A WEEK EARLIER, ON MY final day in Ho Chi Minh City, I rode on the back of a stranger's motorbike. He told me he could take me where I wanted to go.

We zipped through the street traffic, weaving in between other vehicles, stopping and starting, letting some in and cutting others off. We followed the natural rhythm of a roaring chaos. Travelling together, each vehicle reacted to those around it, sensitive to every movement and swerve, intention and desire. A shoal of wheels and exhaust pipes moving forward.

The wind made a parachute of my shirt. I was falling horizontally, plunging not through space but through permeable time. Up ahead, among a crowd of youngsters not old enough to remember war, I spotted the broad shoulders of a thin man I recognized. He was wearing a white button-up that looked newly pressed, sleeves rolled up to the elbow. His arms extended to reach the handlebars of his motorbike. On his feet were a pair of brown leather sandals. Behind him a young woman with long black hair sat sidesaddle. She was wearing a white áo dài, whose top panel fluttered like a flag. She wrapped both arms around his torso and gently placed the side of her face on his arched back.

Holding the edge of my seat, I asked the driver to go faster. I wanted to follow them. I wanted to know where they were going.

But as the motorbike picked up speed, and I blinked, the couple disappeared. Maybe they'd made a sudden turn. Or decided to take a different route. Maybe they were not real. Were never real to begin with. Maybe they were simply two people who shared a brief time together on this earth.

A few minutes passed, and I was about to resign myself to their disappearance. But still I couldn't stop extending my neck to search for them. It was the only thing I could do. We crossed a small bridge, and that was when they floated into my field of vision again, a swerve of a wheel like a magic trick. I patted the driver on the back, to say, *Go, go. Catching up with these two people means everything to me.*

The driver revved his motor and kicked the engine into another gear. He inched closer, and then even closer. As he made one final push, I reached my arm out to catch, with the tips of my fingers, just a sliver of white cloth hanging in the air.

ACKNOWLEDGMENTS

A BOOK IS A FAMILY house others have built for the author to dwell in.

I thank my incredible editor at HarperCollins Canada, Janice Zawerbny, for her wisdom, generosity, and guidance. Thanks to Dan Smetanka and Yukiko Tominaga at Counterpoint Press for believing in this book.

My agent Emmy Nordstrom Higdon, and the folks at Westwood Creative, made bringing this book into the world possible. Editors who showed early support include Jen Sookfong Lee, Anita Chong, Simon Thibault, and Susan Renouf.

Pamela Mulloy is a CanLit treasure, and I'm so fortunate to call her a friend and mentor. Learning from Eva-Lynn Jagoe made me realize writing creatively was possible. Walks with Souvankham Thammavongsa are sources of inspiration. I look up to Barbara Tran in all things. Asha Jeffers and Pacinthe Mattar are my unconditional cheerleaders. Ann Baranowski listened. Thanks to Nam Phi Dang for the friendship and the photos.

I'm enormously grateful for the people who've read and commented on previous versions of the manuscript: Irfan Ali, Edgar Gomez, Doretta Lau, Lili Loofbourow, Kyo Maclear, Pamela Mulloy, Christopher B. Patterson, Danny Ramadan, Souvankham Thammavongsa, and Nandini Thiyagarajan. My writing has benefited from the amazing editors at literary journals. They include Laurie D. Graham and the fantastic team at *Brick*, Vivian Li at *PRISM international*, Iain Higgins at the *Malahat Review*, and Kate O'Gorman at *Grain*. Thanks to Liz Johnston and John Sweet for their meticulous eyes.

I'm fortunate to be a part of various writerly communities. The incredible crew at the *New Quarterly* and Wild Writers Festival welcomed me with open arms. Colleagues at the *Hamilton Review of Books* are a special bunch. The lovely people at Lambda Literary Retreat, particularly Noam Keim and Liana Fu, provided care during a difficult time. The month at the Historic Joy Kogawa House was generative (thanks, Ann-Marie Metten and Johnny Trinh). The Writers' Union of Canada's BIPOC Writers Connect Conference was a wonderful opportunity. The supportive folks at the Humber Summer Workshop (Joselyn Keeshig, Jason Nadon, Sarah Papple, Ele Pawelski, and Canya Selvakumar) helped sustain my writing. Spending two weeks in Lisbon with the wonderful writers at DISQUIET International (Toby Buck, Sharon Davis, Jane Dykema, Donna Knipp, Jess Rezendes, Megan Rich, Krystle May Statler, Mary

Alice Stewart, Veronica Tang, and Margaret Wachs) was a dream.

The Canada Council for the Arts, Ontario Arts Council, Toronto Arts Council, Renison University College, and the University of Waterloo generously provided funding while I was writing this book.

Friends who've supported this journey include Cheryl Narumi Naruse, Dalia Kandiyoti, Rachel Mettler, Himani Bannerji, Chris Webb, Adrie Naylor, Rossana Tudo, Thy Phu, Mary O'Connor, Imre Szeman, Elspeth Brown, Madeleine Thien, David Chariandy, Yen Le Espiritu, Richard Fung, Tim McCaskell, Radhika Mongia, Asha Varadharajan, Monique Truong, Gökbige Tanyildiz, Heather Lambert, and countless others.

I wish Y-Dang Troeung and Don Goellnicht were here to share my joy. I think of them always.

I cherish my father's siblings Cô Yến, Chú Ân, Chú Bão, and Cô Hồng, and their families, now more than ever.

The foundation: my siblings Anh Văn, Chị Trang, Chị Như, Anh Chánh, and Chi Linda, my nieces Rachel, Caitlyn, and Clarissa, and my nephew Brandon.

My father. My mother

My love, Gökbörü.

© Nam Phi Dang

VINH NGUYEN is a writer and educator whose work has appeared in *Brick, Literary Hub, The Malahat Review, PRISM international, Grain, Queen's Quarterly, Current,* and MUBI's *Notebook.* He is a nonfiction editor at *The New Quarterly,* where he curates an ongoing series on refugee, migrant, and diasporic writing. He is the editor of the academic books *Refugee States: Critical Refugee Studies in Canada* and *The Routledge Handbook of Refugee Narratives,* and the author of *Lived Refuge: Gratitude, Resentment, Resilience.* His writing has been short-listed for a National Magazine Award and has received the John Charles Polanyi Prize in Literature. In 2022, he was a Lambda Literary Fellow in Nonfiction for emerging LGBTQ writers. He lives in Toronto, Canada. Find out more at vinhnguyen.ca.